Homeland Security:
Best Practices for
Local Government

Edited by Roger L. Kemp

International
City/County
ICMA
Management
Association
icma.org

ICMA is the professional and educational organization for chief appointed management executives in local government. The purposes of ICMA are to strengthen the quality of local government through professional management and to develop and disseminate new approaches to management through training programs, information services, and publications.

For further information about the publications or services for local governments offered by ICMA, write to Publications Department, ICMA, 777 North Capitol St., N.E., Suite 500, Washington, D.C. 20002. To order publications, call 800/745-8780 (outside the United States, call 770/442-8631, ext. 377) or visit the ICMA Bookstore online at http://bookstore.icma.org.

Library of Congress Cataloging-in-Publication Data

Homeland security : best practices for local government/edited by
Roger L. Kemp.
    p. cm.
  ISBN 0-87326-136-4
 1. Emergency management—United States. 2. Terrorism—United
States--Prevention. 3. Civil defense—United States. 4. Local
government--United States. I. Kemp, Roger L. II. International
City/County Management Association.
  HV551.3.H66 2003
  363.1'056'068—dc21

2003011026

ISBN: 0-87326-136-4

Printed in the United States of America.

07 06 05 04 03

5 4 3 2 1

Design: Will Kemp

Contents

Acknowledgments

The editor and ICMA are grateful to the following organizations and publishers for granting permission to reprint the material contained in this volume. The volume also includes materials from the Federal Emergency Management Agency, the Congressional Research Service, and the Office of Homeland Security.

A.J. Parrino & Associates, Ltd. (*Homeland Protection Professional*)

Bobit Publishing Company (*Police*)

Fire Engineering

International Association of Chiefs of Police (*The Police Chief*)

National Fire Protection Association (*NFPA Journal*)

PRIMEDIA Business Magazines and Media, Inc. (*American City & County* and *Fire Chief*)

Part I

Introduction

1 Best practices in homeland security

Roger L. Kemp

The United States, indeed the world, was shocked on September 11, 2001, when high-jacked commercial jets in well-planned terrorist attacks flew into the Pentagon near our nation's capital and the World Trade Center towers in New York City. Another plane en route to San Francisco crashed in rural southwest Pennsylvania, diverted from its mission apparently by the heroic acts of passengers on board. National security experts believed that this plane was headed for Washington, D.C. The loss of life caused by the planes was the largest on American soil from a war-like incident since the Civil War. Specifically,

American Airlines Flight 11, from Boston, Massachusetts, to Los Angeles, California, crashed into the north tower of the World Trade Center with 92 people on board.

United Airlines Flight 175, also en route from Boston to Los Angeles, crashed into the south tower of the World Trade Center with 65 people on board.

American Airlines Flight 77, flying from Washington, D.C., to Los Angeles, crashed into the Pentagon with 64 people on board.

Finally, *United Airlines Flight 93*, going from Newark, New Jersey, to San Francisco, California, crashed in Shanksville, Pennsylvania, in Somerset County with 44 people on board.

Citizens of the United States, as well as other countries throughout the world, watched in disbelief and horror as television replayed the devastation. America's police and firefighters immediately assumed the role of first responders to these disasters. Cities and counties, and their public safety personnel, established emergency operations centers and incident command posts, deploying all of the resources at their disposal to help the wounded and recover the dead. Months later, after arduous recovery operations, the death toll totaled nearly 3,000 people from all walks of life, including police, fire, and other emergency personnel.

What was amazing was that local governments—cities and counties—were the first responders to these incidents, not the Army, Air Force, Navy, or other branches of the military. Citizens throughout the nation watched as local public safety employees—police and fire personnel—rushed to these accident scenes to limit the loss of life and property. Mayors, county managers, city managers, health officials, public safety line employees, and public utility workers all responded in New York City, Arlington, Virginia, and rural Pennsylvania.

The terrorist acts described above launched a new wave of effort by cities, counties, and states throughout the country to enhance their emergency management programs. Specifically, local, state, and federal officials have focused on four primary phases of emergency management: mitigation, preparedness, response, and recovery:

Mitigation. Mitigation includes efforts to prevent man-made or natural disasters or to lessen their effects. It involves an assessment of the threats facing a community, such as the likelihood of a terrorist attack, and an assessment of possible targets. This is an ongoing process, with continual reassessments as necessary to ensure proper preparedness by local officials.

Preparedness. City and county officials must be prepared to respond properly to disasters of all types, including terrorist acts. Preparedness includes proper planning, resource allocation, training, and simulated disaster response exercises. It is important to conduct exercises to ensure that skills, equipment, and other resources can be effectively coordinated when an emergency occurs. Exercises also provide a good opportunity to identify organizational and departmental shortcomings and take corrective action before an actual event takes place.

Response. A local government's response to a man-made or natural disaster has many components. If possible, the jurisdiction must issue appropriate warnings to the public and keep citizens informed. Donations from the public must be accepted and managed. Mass care and sheltering may also be necessary, depending upon the type and magnitude of the disaster. Proper incident management and coordination are essential. Emergency services and medical care must be provided. Other important aspects of the response phase include search and rescue operations, evacuations according to established procedures, damage assessments, and the proper handling of fatalities.

Recovery. After a natural or man-made disaster, including a terrorist act, the clean-up of debris, the restoration of the environment, the reinstitution of public services, and the rebuilding of the public infrastructure are all necessary to restore civic life. This phase also typically includes disaster assistance, for both citizens and their governments, and crisis counseling, for both civilian and public safety employees.

Local government personnel from numerous departments are involved in these four aspects of emergency management: executive-level management personnel, public safety employees, public health officials, public works employees, and public utilities personnel. Figure 1-1 shows the city and county departments that are typically involved in homeland security operations and issues.

This volume describes best practices in homeland security that have emerged since September 11, 2001. The case studies selected are organized according to the four phases of emergency management. Many of the selections touch on more than one area as Figure 1-2 shows. The practices represented by the case studies listed in Figure 1-2 include the use of new technologies, state-of-the-art computer software, new information-sharing techniques, safer ways to design public buildings, proper evacuation procedures for buildings—both public and private—and ways to improve dispatch services and emergency operations centers. New practices in the nation's capital, as well as the federal government, are also included in this volume.

Figure 1-1.
City and county departments typically involved in homeland security.

Cities (for incorporated areas)	Counties (for unincorporated areas)
City manager	County manager
Fire	Fire
Health	Health
Police	Sheriff
Public utilities	Public utilities
Public works	Public works

Note: The functions of local governments and names of departments vary from state to state (for example, two states, Connecticut and Rhode Island, have no county governments). Some services may also be provided by special districts or private utility companies.

Figure 1-2.

Best practices in homeland security by phases of emergency management.

Case study (selection number)	Phases of Emergency Management			
	Mitigation	Preparedness	Response	Recovery
Emergency management and civil defense (2)	X	X	X	X
Federal assistance (3)	X	X	X	X
Intelligence gathering and networking (4)	X	X	X	
Information sharing by local agencies (5)	X	X	X	X
Community threat assessment (6)	X	X	X	
Preventing terrorist acts (7)	X	X		
Traffic law enforcement (8)	X	X		
Incident responsibility and accountability (9)		X	X	X
Emergency operations centers (10)	X	X	X	X
Design of public buildings (11)	X	X		
Security for public utilities (12)	X	X		
Evacuation planning (13)	X	X	X	
Public works personnel as first responders (14)		X	X	X
Automated public notification systems (15)		X	X	
Geographic information systems (16)	X	X	X	X
Dispatch center services (17)		X	X	
Search and rescue assistance (18)			X	X
Stress management for police officers (19)		X	X	X
Stress management for firefighters (20)	X	X		X
Line-of-duty deaths (21)		X	X	X
The local role in fighting terrorism (22)	X	X	X	
U.S. Homeland Security Advisory System (23)	X	X	X	
Number of cases	15	21	17	11

Note: The cases in this volume frequently encompass more than one phase of emergency management, but they are categorized in the Table of Contents according to their primary focus.

The examples have been taken from 14 states and the District of Columbia. They reflect initiatives in 18 cities, boroughs, and townships and in 12 county governments (see Figure 1-3). Local governments of all population sizes are represented. They range from small communities (such as Anniston, Alabama; Elmira and Hempstead, New York; St. Helens, Oregon; and the township of Washington, Indiana) to larger cities (Cincinnati, Ohio; Los Angeles, San Diego, and San Francisco, California; Milwaukee, Wisconsin; New York City; Oklahoma City; and Phoenix, Arizona). The income levels and politics in those jurisdictions vary widely as well. In many cases, city and county personnel have worked jointly to improve their emergency management operations.

One selection, "Federal Assistance to State and Local Governments," describes new federal grant programs in the area of homeland security. These grant programs are broken down into six areas for ease of reference: emergency management and planning; training; equipment; law enforcement; public health and medical community; and community preparedness. Numerous newly created federal grant programs are included in each of these categories. These grant programs are provided by the Federal Emergency Management Agency (FEMA), the U.S. Fire Administration, the Department of Health and Human Services, the Department of Justice, the Federal Bureau of Investigation, the Department of Energy, and the Department of Defense.

The last selection, "The Future of Homeland Security," takes stock of evolving best practices in the field, categorizes them by the four phases of emergency management (i.e., mitigation, preparedness, response, and recovery), and suggests where homeland security practices should be improved in the future.

Figure 1-3.
Best practices in
homeland security by
type of government.

Cities	Counties	Other
Anniston, Alabama	Arlington County, Virginia	District of Columbia
Bowling Green, Kentucky	Chemung County, New York	
Cincinnati, Ohio	Fairfax County, Virginia	
Elmira, New York	Kanawha County, West Virginia	
Hempstead, New York	Los Angeles County, California	
Long Island, New York (borough)	Montgomery County, Maryland	
Los Angeles, California	Nassau County, New York	
Milwaukee, Wisconsin	Prince George's County, Maryland	
New York, New York	San Diego County, California	
Newport News, Virginia	San Francisco County, California	
Oklahoma City, Oklahoma	Seminole County, Florida	
Palm Beach, Florida	Warren County, Kentucky	
Phoenix, Arizona		
St. Helens, Oregon		
San Diego, California		
San Francisco, California		
San Jose, California		
Washington, Indiana (township)		

Finally, eight appendices are included in this volume. They include the latest information from FEMA on terrorism preparedness and response, the ten steps in the federal disaster declaration process, a listing of the ten FEMA regional offices, a complete directory of the state offices and agencies of emergency management, an evolving lexicon of homeland security-related acronyms, a detailed listing of homeland security Internet resources, a list of the agencies that will become part of the Department of Homeland Security, and an example of a local response to a heightened level of security risk under the Homeland Security Advisory System.

Spurred to action by the events of September 11, 2001, local governments developed the practices described in this volume rapidly—in less than two years. These practices will continue to evolve in cities and counties throughout the United States in response to citizen expectations and directives at the federal level from the new Cabinet-level Department of Homeland Security. The purpose of this volume is to pull together the best practices in homeland security that have evolved so far and present this information in a format that is useful to city and county managers throughout the nation.

2 Emergency management and civil defense

By David Wagman

On Sept. 10, 2001, the Los Angeles Emergency Preparedness Department held a bioterrorism training exercise, one of several disaster drills the agency regularly holds. The reporters who covered the exercise on that Monday could have fit into a telephone booth, recalls Ellis Stanley, the department's general manager.

Today, similar training exercises are media circuses wherever they are held. The attention marks one of the subtle, yet fundamental, shifts in how emergency management goes about its business in the post–Sept. 11 world.

The heightened emphasis on preparing to deal with terrorist threats since Sept. 11 is returning emergency management to its roots in the Civil Defense days of the '40s, '50s and '60s. During those years, Civil Defense efforts involved community vigilance and local preparation to guard against the perceived threat of foreign invasion. As worry over that threat waned, emergency management focused more on natural disaster planning and recovery. That focus was codified with the creation of the Federal Emergency Management Agency (FEMA) in 1979.

The Pope and Timothy McVeigh

The first World Trade Center attack in February 1993 and security efforts to protect Pope John Paul II during his visit to the United States later that year, however, prompted a nearly decade-long effort by emergency managers to make terrorist attacks a part of their disaster planning regimen. The sense of urgency grew after the 1995 Oklahoma City and 1996 Olympic Park bombings, and the 1995 sarin nerve gas attack on the Tokyo subway. The September 2001 attacks in New York City and Washington, D.C., closed the circle, bringing civil defense and terrorism planning once again to the forefront of emergency management planning.

"We're back to where we started," Stanley says.

Well, almost. For one thing, today's terrorist threats are technologically more sophisticated and more difficult to anticipate than those of a generation ago. Where Civil Defense wardens of the '60s might have stood watch on a beach on a dark night to guard against commandos landing in a rubber boat, emergency management teams today plan for and train to respond to terrorism that might come in many different forms, from chemical or biological to nuclear. In a worrisome twist on the rubber raft scenario, for example, emergency managers today must think about the possibility of a nuclear device being packed into a cargo container and loaded onto a ship sailing for a U.S. harbor.

The task of guarding against such a varied menu of threats requires a level of coordination and cooperation that eclipses anything necessary for natural disaster planning. "In the past, our planning was for contingencies we knew a lot about," says Bob

Originally published as "There and Back Again," *Homeland Protection Professional*, Vol. 1, No. 1, pages 28–30, July/August, 2002. Published by A. J. Parrino & Associates, Western Springs, Illinois. Reprinted with permission of the publisher.

Andrews, president of the International Association of Emergency Managers (IAEM) and head of the Clark County, Nev., emergency management department. Tornadoes, hurricanes and floods have predictable seasons and lend themselves to early preparation.

Not so terrorism, which is most effective when it plays on unknown whens, wheres and hows. "We now have to focus on an unknown equation," Andrews says.

New ties to law enforcement

In their quest to deal with those unknowns, emergency managers have a tool, law enforcement, that they lack in dealing with natural disasters. "There's no crime in a flood; there's no investigation or intelligence gathering," says Bob Brooks, who heads up Colorado's emergency management effort as director of the state's Department of Local Affairs. Since Sept. 11, criminal law enforcement and investigation functions have increasingly become part of the emergency management strategy, another fundamental shift in the emergency management system.

"We have a heightened need to work with public safety," Brooks says. His department has staff members assigned to work with the Colorado Bureau of Investigation, which, in turn, has direct links to the FBI. In the fall of 2001, Gov. Bill Owens created a state office to parallel the newly created federal Homeland Security office; Brooks has assigned staff to that office as well.

"If a building falls down, it doesn't matter if it was caused by a bomb, an earthquake or a tornado," Brooks says. "If it was caused by a terrorist, then the added element is the crime scene investigation. It's the same response training, but supplemented by law enforcement."

The communications quandary

Yet even as emergency management evolves to incorporate the threat of terrorism, some things remain constant, notably communications problems. Those problems extend to communications at all levels, whether between emergency agencies that respond to a disaster, or among entities competing for grant money.

"Where every mission fails is in communication," says Mike Fagel, an emergency management director in suburban Chicago and a member of the Illinois Terrorism Task Force.

For Stanley, the communication issue comes down to interoperability: the ability of fire, police, EMS and other teams to talk with one another at the scene of a disaster. Emergency agencies tend to buy their own communications equipment, and much of it doesn't work across agency boundaries. Consequently, communications can break down, hindering emergency response efforts.

Emergency managers are looking to the Federal Communications Commission (FCC) to create a public safety band spectrum that would facilitate interagency communication. However, they realize that the cost of creating a single communication system accessible by all local emergency response units will be steep. In Los Angeles alone, the price tag for changing all fire department radios could run as high as $50 million, Stanley says.

Improving communication between local emergency response departments and state and federal agencies could be tougher still because of the array of agencies involved in terrorism response. For example, since Sept. 11, emergency managers have begun working more closely with local hospitals and healthcare providers, says Marcus Aurelius, emergency management coordinator for Phoenix and co-chair of IAEM's terrorism subcommittee.

Local laws also are being reviewed to clarify everything from line of succession (if local leaders are incapacitated) to who is authorized to impose a quarantine. Efforts also are under way to address potential vulnerabilities in local utilities and pipelines.

Additionally, emergency managers are working with local businesses to help them understand how to survive a terrorist attack, Aurelius says. Realizing the importance of post-attack economic continuity, they're developing ways to help local businesspeople learn how to maintain their businesses after an incident, as well as how to plan for and recover from a disaster.

Budget issues

Lack of funding for emergency management remains a serious issue, with the recent economic downturn squeezing budgets even as the public expects higher levels of preparation. Part of the problem is that Congress had focused its spending priorities on school violence rather than on terrorism, says Karen Cobuluis, a spokeswoman for the National Emergency Management Association, which focuses on statewide response issues. To adjust to the post–Sept. 11 world, Congress has had to reshuffle its budget priorities.

...President Bush and Congress have promised billions of dollars for homeland defense.... Stanley cautions that even after the money becomes available, local emergency managers will need to apply for and compete with other agencies for funds. The money also will likely be earmarked for specific items such as equipment or training.

But specifying exactly how the money can be spent can cause problems, Aurelius says, comparing the situation to a car buyer who's forced to use specific funds for various parts: He can buy tires only with money from a certain pot and must use a separate source of cash to buy the horn.

Emergency management lobbying groups are working to convince Congress of the efficacy of funding entire programs, rather than creating a piecemeal approach. "Congress needs to think how money is allocated at the local level," Aurelius says.

Groups like the National Emergency Management Association (NEMA) also are watching to see how the federal money is allocated. If it's tagged for disbursement generally through the Department of Justice (DOJ), then municipal police and fire organizations stand to benefit the most. If the money is dispersed more through FEMA, it's likely to be targeted at statewide terrorism planning efforts.

Cobuluis prefers the latter scenario. "Cities don't always coordinate with one another on their purchases," she says, arguing that states could better make the spending decisions that benefit multiple jurisdictions.

"A lively period"

Still, emergency managers like to point out that the first response to a terrorist attack is almost always a local one. "All disasters are local; that's the byword we have to remember," says Fagel.

In Colorado, where Brooks' agency provides $120 million a year in grants, the focus is on helping local emergency managers prepare for and respond to disasters, including terrorism. "In a disaster, the response is at a local level when fire, police and ambulance crews work on their own for at least the first few hours," Brooks says. "When they need more help, our folks go in and make immediate connections."

In that sense, the concept of all-hazard disaster planning seems even more relevant than ever. When emergency response crews turn on their sirens and head to a disaster, they need the same level of preparation whether the disaster is caused by nature or, as Aurelius says, by "some bizarre man-created incident."

The process of shoring up homeland defense can bolster the strategies needed to deal with natural disasters, says IAEM's Andrews. A communication system that fosters interoperability, for example, is useful regardless of the nature of a disaster. "We need to develop in a manner that bridges both worlds," he says.

Being an emergency manager on Sept. 12, 2001, wasn't the same as being one on Sept. 10. Since Sept. 11, the job requires emergency managers to continue to plan for and be able to respond to natural disasters, even as they plan for bigger catastrophes.

Emergency planning remains uneven across the country, an indication that it reflects local needs, budget priorities and politics. Regions that are routinely affected by natural disasters are better prepared to respond to a terrorist threat than are "disaster-deficient" parts of the country, Aurelius says. Additionally, areas that have existing regional emergency planning boards are likely to be better able to handle difficult coordination issues if only because they have a core of people who know one another.

Finally, the challenge of embracing national goals and programs related to homeland security and making them work at the local level remains. Sept. 11 spawned a sea change in the concept of emergency management, and the pace of change has yet to slow down. "It is," says Aurelius in a classic understatement, "a lively period."

3 | Federal assistance to state and local governments

Ben Canada

This report lists and describes selected federal programs that assist states and localities in preparing for terrorist attacks, particularly those involving weapons of mass destruction. Some of the programs are authorized specifically for this purpose, while others are general assistance programs that recipients *may* use for terrorism preparedness. Depending on the structure of the program, local governments seeking assistance may apply directly to the federal agency or to the state program administrator.

Preparedness programs are administered by several agencies, including the Departments of Defense, Justice, and Health and Human Services, and the Federal Emergency Management Agency (FEMA). These agencies provide grants, training, and technical assistance for a wide range of preparedness activities. The programs fall into the following categories:

- Emergency management and planning
- Training
- Equipment
- Law enforcement
- Public health and medical community
- Community preparedness.

In creating the Department of Homeland Security, the 107th Congress transferred program responsibilities among agencies. Of the agencies offering terrorism preparedness assistance, the new department will integrate FEMA in its entirety, as well as selected offices from the Departments of Justice and Health and Human Services. Other preparedness programs will remain in their current location. This report reflects any changes in program administration. It will be updated as relevant programs are created, modified, or terminated.

Information in this selection

For each program, this catalog provides the program title, brief description, administering agency, agency phone number, and web site. For those programs registered in the *Catalog of Federal Domestic Assistance* (CFDA), the program number is provided after the title. This catalog provides only basic descriptive and contact information about the selected programs, and does not provide details about course offerings and application requirements.

For more descriptive information on a specific program as well as application deadlines and requirements, please see the CFDA web site at http://www.cfda.gov. The most up-to-date information, however, is available on agency and program web sites.

Originally published as *Terrorism Preparedness: Catalog of Selected Federal Assistance Programs*, CRS Report for Congress RL31227, Congressional Research Service, Library of Congress, Washington, D.C., January 6, 2003.

Federal agency training catalogs

Federal agencies have published catalogs with detailed information about their terrorism training programs. Agency catalogs typically provide descriptions of specific training courses and technical assistance programs, give application requirements, and often offer suggestions for writing grant proposals. The following federal agency catalogs are available on the Internet:

- *Compendium of Weapons of Mass Destruction Courses*—Descriptions of all federal training programs for responding to weapons of mass destruction. Available at: http://www.usfa.fema.gov/dhtml/fire-service/cwmdc.cfm.

- *Office for Domestic Preparedness: Weapons of Mass Destruction Training Program*—Detailed information on training programs offered by the Department of Justice's Office for Domestic Preparedness. Available at: http://www.ojp.usdoj.gov/odp/docs/coursecatalog.pdf.

Grant writing assistance

Grant applicants may seek assistance from a number of sources. All applicants should consult the federal agency to which they are applying. Many federal agencies provide grant writing assistance and workshops tailored to the specific requirements of their applications. Applicants might also consult with an appropriate state agency (such as the state department of emergency services or public health). Some state agencies provide technical assistance for completing federal grant applications and, in some instances, may even submit the grant on behalf of a locality.

Listed below are Congressional Research Service (CRS) products and other resources available through the Internet that may assist applicants in completing applications.

- *CRS Grants Information web page*—This web site for congressional staff links to key grants sources, including the *Catalog of Federal Domestic Assistance*, various federal pages intended specifically to assist grant seekers, and the Foundation Center for private foundation funding. It also links to the web pages on writing and developing grant proposals (see below). Available at: http://www.crs.gov/reference/general/grantsinfo.shtml.

- *Catalog of Federal Domestic Assistance*—The CFDA includes an instructional page, *Developing and Writing Grant Proposals*, to assist federal grant seekers. Available at: http://www.cfda.gov/public/cat-writing.htm.

- *Foundation Center Proposal Writing Short Course*—Online tutorial for learning how to develop good grant proposals. Available at: http://fdncenter.org/learn/shortcourse/prop1.html.

Related CRS products

For more information on federal programs and policy issues related to state and local emergency preparedness, please see the following CRS products:

CRS Report RS21302, *Assistance to Firefighters Program*, by Len Kruger.

CRS Report RL31490, *Department of Homeland Security: State and Local Preparedness Issues*, by Ben Canada.

CRS Report RS21227, *Emergency Management Assistance Compact (EMAC): An Overview*, by Ben Canada.

CRS Report RS21377, *Federal Emergency Warning Systems: An Overview*, by Shawn Reese.

CRS Report RL31475, *First Responder Initiative: Issues and Options*, by Ben Canada.

CRS Report RL31680, *Homeland Security: Standards for State and Local Preparedness*, by Ben Canada.

CRS Report RL31670, *Transfer of FEMA to the Department of Homeland Security: Issues for Congressional Oversight*, by Keith Bea.

CRS Report RL31465, *Protecting Critical Infrastructure from Terrorist Attack: A Catalog of Selected Federal Assistance Programs*, coordinated by John Moteff.

CRS Report RL31263, *Public Health Security and Bioterrorism Preparedness and Response Act (P.L. 107-188): Provisions and Changes to Preexisting Law*, by C. Stephen Redhead, Donna U. Vogt, and Mary E. Tiemann.

CRS Report RS21348, *Risk Assessment in the President's National Strategy for Homeland Security*, by Rob Buschmann.

CRS Report RL31266, *State and Local Preparedness for Terrorism: Selected Policy Issues*, by Ben Canada.

CRS Report RS20071, *United States Fire Administration: An Overview*, by Len Kruger.

CRS Report RS21073, *Urban Search and Rescue Task Forces: Fact Sheet*, by Ben Canada.

CRS Terrorism Briefing Book: http://www.congress.gov/brbk/html/ebter1.shtml.

FEDERAL PREPAREDNESS PROGRAMS

Emergency management and planning

Emergency Management Institute

Training for state and local emergency response personnel in basic emergency management and terrorism preparedness. The Institute is intended to improve emergency management practices among state and local emergency managers, and federal officials, in response to emergencies and disasters. Programs embody the Comprehensive Emergency Management System by unifying the elements of management common to all emergencies: preparedness, mitigation, response, and recovery. The Institute offers a wide selection of courses. *Note: Pursuant to the Homeland Security Act of 2002 (P.L. 107-296), FEMA and all its component programs, including EMI, will be transferred to the new department.*

Agency:	Federal Emergency Management Agency
Phone:	800-238-3358
Web site:	EMI web site: http://training.fema.gov/emiweb;
	FEMA regional offices and state emergency management offices: http://www.fema.gov/regions/index.shtm
CFDA:	83.527, 83.529, 83.530z

Emergency Management Performance Grants (EMPG)

Grants to states to develop comprehensive emergency management plans, including plans to manage consequences of terrorist attacks. The program's goal is to improve overall emergency planning, preparedness, mitigation, response, and recovery capabilities. FEMA has identified 13 emergency management functions for which states are encouraged, but not required, to use EMPG funds. These functions are: (1) laws and authorities; (2) hazard identification and risk assessment; (3) hazard mitigation; (4) resource management; (5) planning; (6) direction, control, and coordination; (7) communications and warning; (8) operations and procedures; (9) logistics and facilities; (10) training; (11) exercises, evaluations, and corrective actions; (12) crisis communications, public education, and information; and (13) finance and administration. *Note: When FEMA is transferred to the new Department of Homeland Security, this program will also be transferred.*

Agency:	Federal Emergency Management Agency
Phone:	202-646-3792
Web site:	http://www.usfa.fema.gov/dhtml/inside-usfa/cfda83552.html
CFDA:	83.552

National Fire Academy

Training for state and local emergency managers to increase the professional level of the fire service and emergency medical service. Courses are offered at the National Fire Academy training facility in Emmitsburg, MD, but also through regional offices and distance learning mechanisms. The Academy offers a wide selection of courses in such areas as professional development, incident management, information management, hazardous materials, fire prevention, and volunteer leadership. *Note: When FEMA is transferred to the new Department of Homeland Security, the Academy will also be transferred.*

Agency:	U.S. Fire Administration (FEMA)
Phone:	800-238-3358 or 301-447-1035
Web site:	http://www.usfa.fema.gov/nfa
CFDA:	83.009, 83.010

Metropolitan Medical Response Systems (MMRS)

Funding to metropolitan areas that upgrade and improve their own planning and preparedness to respond to mass-casualty events. Under contracts with the Department of Health and Human Services (HHS), MMRS participants are required to coordinate and integrate the planning and preparedness efforts of law enforcement, fire, hazmat, emergency medical systems, hospitals, public health, and other local first responders. The participants receive funds in return for delivering to HHS fully integrated plans for training, organization, and response. The funds may be used to buy special equipment and stockpile pharmaceuticals and medical supplies. Through FY2002, HHS had entered into contracts with 122 metropolitan areas. *Note: On March 1, 2003, pursuant to the Homeland Security Act of 2002 (P.L. 107-296), the MMRS program was scheduled to be transferred to the new department.*

Agency:	Office of Emergency Preparedness (HHS/OEP)
Phone:	301-443-1167
Web site:	http://mmrs.hhs.gov
CFDA:	Not listed

Training

Domestic Preparedness Training and Technical Assistance Program

Grants to provide training to state and local jurisdictions to respond to terrorist incidents involving weapons of mass destruction (WMD), such as nuclear, biological, chemical, and explosive devices. The Office for Domestic Preparedness utilizes the capabilities of a number of specialized institutions in the design and delivery of its training programs. These include private contractors, other federal and state agencies, and the National Domestic Preparedness Consortium, among others. *Note: Pursuant to the Homeland Security Act of 2002 (P.L. 107-296), all programs administered by the Office for Domestic Preparedness will be transferred to the new Department of Homeland Security.*

Agency:	Office for Domestic Preparedness (Department of Justice)
Phone:	800-368-6498
Web site:	http://www.ojp.usdoj.gov/odp
CFDA:	16.008

State and local domestic preparedness exercise support

Grants and technical assistance to aid state and local jurisdictions in planning and conducting exercises that simulate response to terrorist attacks involving weapons of mass destruction (WMD). Exercises and simulations may be conducted on a local, regional, state, or national scale. Assistance involves evaluation of the authorities, plans, policies, procedures, and resources used in response operations. ODP provides policy, guidance, standards for scheduling, and uniformity in design, development, conduct, and evaluation of domestic preparedness exercises and related activities. *Note: This program, and all ODP programs, will be transferred to the new Department of Homeland Security.*

Agency:	Office for Domestic Preparedness (Department of Justice)
Phone:	800-368-6498
Web site:	http://www.ojp.usdoj.gov/odp
CFDA:	16.009

First responder counterterrorism training assistance

Grants to states to enhance the capabilities of first responders in managing the consequences of terrorist acts. Training is provided in each of the 50 states through individual state fire training systems. Training is targeted for first responders who will come into contact with and manage the consequences of terrorist acts. *Note: When FEMA is transferred to the new Department of Homeland Security, this program will also be transferred.*

Agency:	U.S. Fire Administration (FEMA)
Phone:	301-447-1533
Web site:	http://www.usfa.fema.gov/dhtml/inside-usfa/cfda83547.html
CFDA:	83.547

State Fire Training System Grants

Financial assistance to states to improve their training capabilities. Grants to states to enhance the capacity of their state-level training system and enable them to deliver a variety of National Fire Academy courses and programs. *Note: When FEMA is transferred to the new Department of Homeland Security, this program will also be transferred.*

Agency:	U.S. Fire Administration (FEMA)
Phone:	301-447-1376
Web site:	http://www.usfa.fema.gov/dhtml/inside-usfa/cfda83553.html
CFDA:	83.553

Equipment

State Domestic Preparedness Equipment Support Program

Grants to states to purchase specialized equipment for responding to terrorist attacks involving weapons of mass destruction (WMD). Grants are distributed to states, which then distribute funds to localities in accordance with pre-approved state plans. Program provides for a comprehensive threat and needs assessment, develops a three-year plan to enhance first responder capabilities, and provides for equipment purchases and the provision of specialized training. *Note: This program, and all ODP programs, will be transferred to the new Department of Homeland Security.*

Agency:	Office for Domestic Preparedness (Department of Justice)
Phone:	800-368-6498
Web site:	http://www.ojp.usdoj.gov/odp
CFDA:	16.007

Hazardous Materials Assistance Program

Grants and technical assistance to plan and train for response to oil and hazardous material incidents. Grants are distributed to states, which may then distribute funds to local or tribal governments. Program seeks to enhance state and local capabilities to operate within the National Response System (NRS) and to support the Comprehensive Hazardous Materials Emergency Response—Capability Assessment Program (CHER-CAP). This program is coordinated by FEMA, the Department of Transportation, and the Environmental Protection Agency. *Note: FEMA will be transferred to the new Department of Homeland Security.*

Agency:	Federal Emergency Management Agency
Phone:	301-447-1009
Web site:	http://www.usfa.fema.gov/dhtml/inside-usfa/cfda83012.html
CFDA:	83.012

Assistance to Fire Fighters Grant Program (FIRE grants)

Grants made directly to fire departments to equip and train firefighters and emergency medical technicians. Program is intended to promote general improvements in firefighter safety and effectiveness, not to directly improve terrorism preparedness. Eligible activities include: establishing fitness programs; buying fire trucks and other vehicles (no more than 25% of the total amount appropriated may be awarded to purchase vehicles); buying firefighting equipment, including equipment for communications and monitoring; buying personal protective equipment; funding fire prevention programs (no less than 5% of the total appropriation). *Note: When FEMA is transferred to the new Department of Homeland Security, this program will also be transferred.*

Agency:	U.S. Fire Administration (FEMA)
Phone:	866-274-0960 or 301-447-1608
Web site:	http://www.usfa.fema.gov/grants
CFDA:	83.554
Other:	For more information, see CRS Report RS21302, Assistance to Firefighters Program

Homeland Defense Equipment Reuse Program

Program offers surplus radiological detection instrumentation to cities. Equipment is "older-generation" instrumentation that would otherwise be destroyed. Recipients can receive equipment training from the Office for Domestic Preparedness.

Agency:	Office of Assets Utilization, Oak Ridge (Department of Energy)
Phone:	865-576-2598
Web site:	http://epic.er.doe.gov/epic/pdfs/hderp_factsheet.pdf
CFDA:	Not listed

Law enforcement

State and local antiterrorism training

Training and technical assistance in terrorism response for state and local law enforcement personnel. Program funds four broad activities: (1) providing state and local law enforcement agencies with knowledge of "political" extremist movements; (2) disseminating information relating to vital elements of law enforcement preparedness for terrorist attacks; (3) providing a general planning orientation to state and local law enforcement pertaining to crisis and consequence management and incident command, including essential elements requisite to conducting criminal investigations and prosecutions of terrorist threats and incidents; and (4) maintaining and enhancing a domestic terrorism database. *Note: This program, and all ODP programs, will be transferred to the new Department of Homeland Security.*

Agency:	Office for Domestic Preparedness (Department of Justice)
Phone:	800-368-6498
Web site:	http://www.ojp.usdoj.gov/odp
CFDA:	16.614

Law enforcement assistance—FBI field police training

Training and technical assistance for state and local law enforcement officials to develop professional skills. Course topics range from basic recruit training to specialized instruction in such areas as fingerprinting, police-community relations, hostage negotiation, white-collar crime, organized crime, computer fraud, management techniques, investigative support, and criminal investigative analysis.

Agency:	Federal Bureau of Investigation (DOJ)
Phone:	Contact field office: http://www.fbi.gov/contact/fo/fo.htm
Web site:	http://www.fbi.gov/hq/td/academy/academy.htm
CFDA:	16.302

Local Law Enforcement Block Grant

Formula grants to support general law enforcement improvements. Funds may be used for a wide variety of activities, including (1) purchasing technology and other equipment directly related to basic law enforcement functions; (2) hiring and training additional law enforcement officers and necessary support personnel; (3) enhancing security at locations that are considered a special risk for incidents of crime, such as schools; and (4) establishing multijurisdictional task forces composed of local, state, and federal law enforcement officials to prevent and control crime.

Agency:	Bureau of Justice Assistance (Department of Justice)
Phone:	888-549-9901, option 4
Web site:	http://www.ojp.usdoj.gov/bja/grant/llebg_app.html
CFDA:	16.592

Public health and medical community

Public health preparedness and response for bioterrorism

Formula grants to the health departments of all 50 states, the District of Columbia, the U.S. territories, and the nation's three largest municipalities (New York, Chicago, and Los Angeles County) to upgrade state and local preparedness for responding to bioterrorism attacks and other public health threats and emergencies. Funding must be used for preparedness planning and readiness assessment, expanding disease surveillance and epidemiologic capacity, strengthening lab capacity, establishing a secure communications network among state and local public health agencies, and education and training.

Agency:	Centers for Disease Control and Prevention (HHS/CDC)
Phone:	770-488-2740
Web site:	http://www.bt.cdc.gov/planning/coopagreementaward
CFDA:	93.283

Bioterrorism Hospital Preparedness Program

Formula grants to the health departments of all 50 states, the District of Columbia, the U.S. territories, and the nation's three largest municipalities (New York, Chicago, and Los Angeles County) to facilitate state and regional planning with local hospitals and other health care facilities, and to upgrade the preparedness of these entities to respond to bioterrorism, natural outbreaks of infectious disease, and other public health emergencies. Funding is used for regional hospital preparedness planning, and to recruit and train emergency personnel and upgrade hospital infrastructure.

Agency:	Health Resources and Services Administration (HHS/HRSA)
Phone:	301-443-4996
Web site:	http://www.hrsa.gov/bioterrorism.htm
CFDA:	93.0033

U.S. Army Medical Research Institute of Infectious Diseases

Training opportunities for public health professionals. Courses are taught at the USAM-RIID facility in Aberdeen, MD, but are also available through satellite broadcasts and other distance learning mechanisms. Courses focus on recognizing signs of bioterrorism attacks, planning and preparing for mass casualties, and preventing spread of disease.

Agency:	U.S. Army Medical Research Institute of Infectious Diseases (Department of Defense)
Phone:	410-436-2230 or 410-436-3393
Web site:	http://www.usamriid.army.mil/education/index.html
CFDA:	Not listed

Community preparedness

Citizen Corps

Civilian volunteer program to assist in emergency planning and response. Includes a number of programs, including Community Emergency Response Teams (CERTs), Volunteers in Police Service (VIPS), Medical Reserve Corps, and Neighborhood Watch. Citizen Corps programs can provide mechanisms for involving civilian volunteers for a variety of purposes, including emergency planning, disaster recovery, and logistical support to first responders. Federal assistance can include equipment, training, technical assistance, and monetary grants. With federal funding, a number of states are also providing training and technical assistance to interested communities. *Note: When FEMA is transferred to the new Department of Homeland Security, this program will also be transferred.*

Agency:	Federal Emergency Management Agency
Phone:	Call state official: http://www.citizencorps.gov/statepoc.html
Web site:	http://www.citizencorps.gov
CFDA:	Not listed

Note: The Congressional Research Service will update this information to reflect the transfer of programs into the new Department of Homeland Security. CRS also will update the information as relevant programs are created, modified, or terminated. CRS provides direct assistance only to members of Congress and their staffs. The best way for the general public to access the most recent information is to go to the web site of the National Association of Counties (NACo), http://www.naco.org. From the home page, access "Homeland Security"; under "Counties and Homeland Security," select "Resources and Best Practices," then "Terrorism Preparedness: Select Federal Assistance

Programs." For more information on policy issues related to state and local preparedness, see the following reports:

CRS Report RL31465, *Protecting Critical Infrastructure from Terrorist Attack: A Catalog of Selected Federal Assistance Programs*, coordinated by John Moteff.

CRS Report RL31475, *First Responder Initiative: Policy Issues and Options*, by Ben Canada.

CRS Report RL31490, *Department of Homeland Security: State and Local Preparedness Issues*, by Ben Canada.

Part II

Mitigation

4 | Intelligence gathering and networking

Matthew J. Hickman and Brian A. Reaves

Following the tragic events of September 11, 2001, and the subsequent focus on homeland security, a new role has emerged for state and local law enforcement. The reality of terrorist "sleepers" living within U.S. borders, combined with the discovery that at least three of the September 11 hijackers had contacts with state and local law enforcement officers in the weeks and months leading up to the attacks, have made it clear that domestic terrorism is increasingly a local concern. State and local agencies are now being asked to play a much larger part in what has traditionally been a federal concern, not only as first responders to terrorist incidents but also as primary gatherers of intelligence.

The ability to quickly compile, process, and disseminate intelligence about persons and groups is critical to the maintenance of homeland security. Primary intelligence sources include federal, state, local, and international law enforcement bodies. In order to assist state and local law enforcement in effectively fulfilling this new role, federal funding has been made available (through the USA Patriot Act of 2001) for the development and enhancement of law enforcement information systems relating to terrorism, with a particular emphasis on information sharing.

Key issues for state and local police

This networked approach recognizes that the officer in the field, perhaps by transmitting the details of a seemingly routine traffic stop to a centralized data system, could potentially help avert a national disaster. Some key issues for state and local agencies are (1) the ability to maintain computer records on law enforcement contacts of all kinds, (2) the ability of officers to access and transmit information from the field, (3) the ability to share intelligence among federal, state, and local agencies, and (4) the ability to use that intelligence to identify individuals in a variety of contexts, ranging from a traffic stop to a local sporting event involving thousands of people.

Baseline data from LEMAS survey

In assessing the potential to meet these needs, and in tracking developments in the coming years, some baseline data collected before the September 11 attacks are helpful. At present, the most systematic and comprehensive source of national data on law enforcement personnel, expenditures and pay, operations, equipment, computers and information systems, and policies and procedures is the Law Enforcement Management and Administrative Statistics (LEMAS) program administered by the U.S. Department of Justice, Bureau of Justice Statistics (BJS). The LEMAS surveys provide national estimates for all state and local law enforcement agencies based on a representative sample of

Originally published as "Local Police and Homeland Security: Some Baseline Data." Reprinted from *The Police Chief*, Vol. LXIX, No. 10, pages 83–88, October, 2002. Copyright held by the International Association of Chiefs of Police, 515 North Washington Street, Alexandria, VA 22314 USA. Further reproduction without express written permission from IACP is strictly prohibited.

more than 3,000 agencies. LEMAS surveys have been conducted in 1987, 1990, 1993, 1997, 1999, and 2000.[1]

This selection summarizes LEMAS survey data from 2000 regarding data collection, digital technology, surveillance, communication, and in-field access to information among local police departments in the United States. Data from additional sources are presented where appropriate. These data are presented as a baseline that may be used both to describe the conditions before September 11 and, when compared with future LEMAS data, to track and document subsequent changes in police operations which may be attributable to the September 11 attacks. These data may be useful for planning, budgeting, and policy making at all levels of government.

The analyses are limited to local police departments (to include county, municipal, tribal, and regional police). This is not intended to minimize the role of sheriffs' offices, state law enforcement agencies, or agencies serving special jurisdictions. All law enforcement agencies and their officers play important parts in the maintenance of homeland security. However, an analysis of all state and local agencies would be quite lengthy, and, given that local police departments constitute 71 percent of all state and local agencies and 63 percent of state and local officers and collectively serve more than 205 million residents, it appears that a focus on local police is warranted.

Law enforcement agencies and personnel

In discussing the homeland security role of local police, it is useful to first consider the prevalence of local police departments and officers in the United States. In addition to providing the "numbers," this will help to demonstrate the capacity for local police to serve as a network for intelligence gathering. As of June 2000 there were about 17,800 state and local law enforcement agencies in the United States, employing slightly more than 708,000 full-time sworn officers. There were 12,666 local police departments, employing 440,920 full-time sworn officers.

The majority of local police agencies in the United States are small, with three-quarters of all local agencies employing fewer than 25 full-time officers. However, these agencies represent only 15 percent of all full-time officers. In contrast, only about 5 percent of all local police agencies employ 100 or more officers, but these agencies employ about 61 percent of all full-time officers. Similarly, the majority of local police agencies in the United States serve small populations. About three-quarters of all local agencies serve populations of fewer than 10,000 residents. In contrast, only 3 percent of local agencies serve populations of 100,000 or more residents.

Police contacts with the public

An important measure relevant to the role of local police in homeland security is the extent to which local police officials interact with civilians annually. A baseline measure of the prevalence of contacts between the police and the public is important for tracking future police activity, particularly in light of their new role as primary gatherers of intelligence.

Although LEMAS does not collect such data, the Police-Public Contact Survey (PPCS), a supplement to the National Crime Victimization Survey (NCVS) administered by BJS, provides national estimates of the prevalence and nature of face-to-face contacts between the police and the public. Estimates from the 1999 PPCS indicate that about one in five persons age 16 or older, or roughly 43.8 million people in 1999, had at least one face-to-face contact with a police officer. About half of these contacts, involving 19.3 million drivers, occurred in the context of a motor vehicle stop.

Data concerning face-to-face contacts are particularly relevant in light of known contacts between police and some of the September 11 hijackers (as reported by various news services). For example, in July 2001, Florida police stopped and ticketed hijacker Mohamed Atta for having an invalid driver's license. Atta failed to appear at a required hearing, and police issued a bench warrant for his arrest. Three weeks later, police again stopped Atta for speeding. Unaware of the outstanding warrant, police allowed Atta to proceed with a warning. In August 2001, Virginia police stopped hijacker Hani Hanjour for speeding. In a third incident, just two days before the September 11 attacks, Maryland police stopped and ticketed hijacker Ziad Jarrah for speeding.

Collecting and maintaining data

Another important measure is the extent to which information about police-public contacts is recorded, particularly in an electronic format. Electronic records of these events are crucial to a networked, shared information system. According to LEMAS data, about 70 percent of local police agencies maintained computer records of incident reports and arrests in 2000. Sixty percent maintained computer records of traffic citations and accidents. Less common were computer records of warrants (43 percent), traffic stops (36 percent), and criminal histories (33 percent), although a majority of larger agencies maintained these kinds of records.

In-field access to data

In order to be effective as both gatherers and users of intelligence, officers need to be able to quickly access information resources from the field. LEMAS provides estimates of the extent to which local agencies are using in-field computers for purposes of data access and communication—important technological enhancements for their role in homeland security. About 40 percent of all local police departments in 2000, employing 75 percent of all officers, were using some type of in-field computer or terminal. As might be expected, in-field computers are more common among larger agencies. Almost 90 percent of agencies serving populations of 250,000 or more residents use them.

In-field computers in 2000 were more likely to be used for purposes of data retrieval, as only about one-fifth of all local departments were using in-field computers for communications. Likewise, in about one-fifth of departments, officers could electronically transmit criminal incident reports to a central information system. In about one-quarter of local departments, officers were able to access vehicle records and driving records via in-field computers, and, in about one-sixth of departments, officers could access criminal histories.

Information sharing

An important homeland security function for all law enforcement agencies is to share information with other agencies, both locally and nationally. This baseline measure is perhaps one of the most important to consider. Twenty-eight percent of local police departments in 2000, including three-quarters of all departments serving a population of 250,000 or more residents, used computers for inter-agency information sharing (see Figure 4-1). Agencies serving smaller populations were much less likely to be using

Figure 4-1.
Use of computers by local police departments for interagency information sharing, 2002.

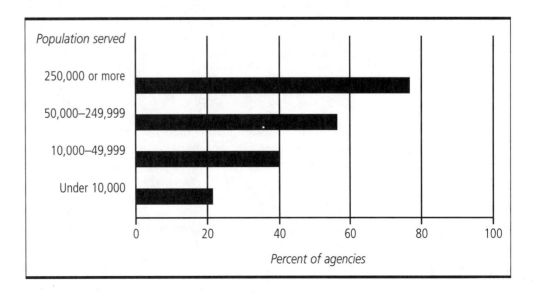

computers for this function, and it is clear that substantial federal assistance for technology enhancement should be directed toward these agencies. Agencies using computers for interagency information sharing employed about half of all officers.

Video technology and digital imaging

A great deal of attention has been focused on the ability to identify individuals using digital imaging and video technology. Video cameras can make a record to identify individuals and place them in a particular time-space context. Of particular interest is the use of video cameras in concert with facial recognition software that takes measurements from digital images and matches them against a database of known or wanted offenders, either in real time or during later review.

An important question is the extent to which local agencies are using these technologies and could potentially contribute to national data resources. According to LEMAS data, nearly half of all local police departments, employing 61 percent of all local police officers, regularly used video cameras in 2000. Overall, local police departments had about 35,000 video cameras in operation.

As might be expected, the most common use of video cameras was in patrol cars. Thirty-seven percent of all local departments in 2000 used video cameras in this application. Thirteen percent of departments, including about one-third of agencies serving 250,000 or more residents, used video cameras for fixed-site surveillance. Nine percent of departments, including one-half of departments serving 250,000 or more residents, used video cameras for mobile surveillance. Finally, 7 percent of local agencies, including 30 percent of those serving 250,000 or more residents, used video cameras for traffic enforcement.

About three in ten local departments, employing 65 percent of all officers, regularly used digital imaging for mug shots. This included more than half of all agencies serving 10,000 or more residents, and about three-quarters of those serving 250,000 or more residents. Provided some level of standardization, these digital images could contribute substantially to national data resources for facial recognition. In addition, 16 percent of local departments, including roughly half of agencies serving 50,000 or more residents, used digital imaging technology for suspect composites. Use of digital imaging in this context increases the ability to quickly disseminate suspect composites to other agencies and may also contribute to facial recognition databases.

Future directions

In the United States, the September 11 terrorist attacks have given rise to a combined federal, state, and local approach to homeland security that greatly expands the state and local role. State and local police are fulfilling a new, enhanced role both as first responders to terrorist incidents and as primary gatherers of intelligence. This selection has provided some baseline data that describe conditions in the field before September 11, and can be used for tracking subsequent developments. What should we expect to see in future data collections?

Given the substantial amount of federal funding authorized by the USA Patriot Act of 2001, we should expect to see significant changes in these baseline measures in future iterations of LEMAS. Specifically, we should expect more widespread use of computers for data collection and information sharing. The Patriot Act authorized $150 million to expand the Regional Information Sharing Systems grant program to help state and local criminal justice agencies combat terrorist conspiracies and activities, and $1.5 billion to expand the Crime Identification Technology Act of 1998 to include grants for criminal justice information system improvements relating to antiterrorism purposes.

We should also expect to see more personnel working in specialized intelligence capacities, as well as the creation of antiterrorism units or inter-agency task forces. The Patriot Act authorized $125 million for grants to state and local governments to hire more law enforcement personnel to serve in intelligence gathering and analysis positions, purchase equipment for intelligence gathering and analysis, provide training on intelligence gathering and analysis, and fund technical assistance programs that focus on inter-agency coordination of intelligence functions.

...In addition, other funding mechanisms are already in place, such as the programs administered by the various components of the U.S. Department of Justice Office of Justice Programs (OJP) as well as the Office of Community Oriented Policing Services (COPS). Finally, the Bush administration's wartime restructuring of governmental functions also ensures that support for antiterrorism efforts will have the highest priority. [For the federal agencies that will be transferred to the Homeland Security Department, see Appendix G.]

Notes

Points of view in this selection are those of the authors and do not necessarily represent the official position of the U.S. Department of Justice, where both authors work in the Bureau of Justice Statistics.

[1] Greater detail on LEMAS can be found at the BJS web site at www.ojp.usdoj.gov/bjs.

5 | Information sharing by local agencies

James Russo and Dennis Labriola

On September 11, 2001, a clarion call sounded throughout the nation and the world. In addition to the obvious spotlight that was cast on the need for heightened alertness and precautions in the face of an unprecedented threat to our national security from determined, faceless terrorists, came a dramatic awareness that had been growing in intensity for several years before that memorable date.

Just about everyone in law enforcement reached the same general conclusion at virtually the same time: the need for the integration and sharing of information among local, regional, and state public safety agencies was no longer an option but in fact had become a new paradigm for our profession. Even though this type of interagency communication is being effectively conducted today on a limited basis, emerging technology is making it possible to establish these networks faster, less expensively, and more effectively than ever before.

The need for improved local communication and information sharing is a concept that many of us in law enforcement understand instinctively, though our typical knee-jerk response to most local incidents or criminal investigations historically has been to "keep it in-house" and to limit "outside involvement." This sort of parochial thinking largely prevailed—until September 11.

No developed system

Consider our venue, Nassau County, Long Island, New York. With 21 separate police agencies, including a 3,000-person county department, spread out over 287 square miles and serving a population of more than one million, the county should have a system for sharing law enforcement information.

Unfortunately, other than a limited county information sharing system, contiguous communities in our county can gather data about events in California or Nebraska more easily (thanks to tie-ins with federal agencies) than they can gather information about one another. For example, a police officer in Hempstead who is suspicious about an individual found lurking near a local school has no easy way of knowing if reports of similar noncriminal behavior were posted in nearby Garden City, Westbury, or Floral Park.

Valuable data available

Naturally, this works both ways. Since 1988 the 112-officer Hempstead Police Department has been equipped with state-of-the-art computer programs storing a wealth of data that could provide surrounding law enforcement agencies with valuable information that could play a vital role in helping them prevent and fight crime—if they could access it.

These include programs such as the Impact ARMS records management system that tracks incident activity, crime reports, warrants, orders of protection, firearm permits, and other critical data, and the Impact VCAD visual computer-aided dispatch system that provides dispatchers and officers in mobile units with current information on location history, hazards, preplans, and geo-based data. Another computer-aided system called PISTOL (photo imaging software technology online) allows us to capture clear digital images of prisoners, suspects, stolen property, and crime scenes that, if made easily available to other departments, could be invaluable.

Fully aware that situations like this exist around the country, Governor Tom Ridge, on assuming his new position as director of the White House Office of Homeland Security in October 2001, said that he expects governments of every size and description to work together, including those supporting local, regional, state, and federal agencies. He called for a new era of interagency cooperation in the fight against crime and terrorism, and the response was a unanimous nod of approval.

IACP demands action

Echoing that call, IACP President Bill Berger called for the creation of a new partnership linking federal, state, and local agencies when he testified before the U.S. Senate's Governmental Affairs Committee on the role of local law enforcement in homeland defense. He noted that the nation's 16,000 state and local law enforcement agencies and their 700,000 officers have an intimate knowledge of the communities they protect and are uniquely qualified to serve as the first line of defense against terrorism and other criminal acts.

Berger also pointed out that the underpinning of this strategy depends on the timely sharing, analysis and dissemination of critical information between these departments. In March 2001, the IACP and the Office of Community Oriented Policing Services convened a two-day national summit on intelligence identification, collection, analysis, sharing and use. The goal of this meeting was to promote the development and sharing of intelligence among all law enforcement agencies, as well as to lay the groundwork for developing a structure for information exchange.

Before September 11, a number of states—including Utah, Kansas, and Oklahoma, as well as our neighbor to the north, Canada—already had developed task forces and programs to ensure a greater sharing of pertinent information among various public safety agencies operating within their jurisdictions.

In January 2002, New York Governor George Pataki announced the creation of a statewide program to link more than 580 local police agencies with each other, as well as with state and federal authorities, in a communications network.

Data sharing in Chemung

One New York county that serves as a good example of what can be done when local agencies pull together is Chemung, which lies midway between New York City and Buffalo. In 1994 the Chemung County Office of Fire and Emergency Management linked six local municipalities—including the city of Elmira—in a new computer-aided dispatch and record management system. Since then, more than 150 officers who cover the county's 412 square miles have relied on the system around the clock to provide security for 96,000 residents.

Providing a wide range of data relating to people, addresses, vehicles, warrants, orders of protection, and more, that system would cost between $250,000 and $500,000 to build today. The technology behind this Impact system is known as a wide area network, or WAN. It consists of a number of primary and backup computers, special software, and a central database at a county facility, all linked by phone lines. According to Thomas Pesesky, deputy director of the Chemung County Office of Fire and Emergency Management, the system has operated very efficiently since its installation and recently was instrumental in helping to apprehend several burglary suspects involved in a three-county pursuit.

Other regional programs

In addition, the Regional Information Sharing Systems (RISS) program is designed to assist state and local agencies. With six centers, RISS shares information and intelligence regarding terrorism. Regional databases maintained by the high intensity drug trafficking areas (HIDTAs) primarily function to fight the illegal drug trade but also are useful as intelligence-sharing sources.

Another welcome step in this direction was the announcement of the FBI's new state and local advisory board and the creation of its new law enforcement coordinator.

Undoubtedly, law enforcement administrators throughout the United States are universally hailing these long-overdue moves toward greater interagency cooperation and information sharing. At the same time, we have no doubt these same pragmatic executive officers are questioning how such cooperation can best be achieved in their jurisdictions and at what cost.

We believe the answers to these questions are relatively easy and are becoming more practical and viable thanks to today's fast-changing technology. The system outlined in this selection costs a fraction of many of those now in use but has the same or greater efficiency. In addition, it is hardly news that funding for projects like this is included in the $38 billion antiterrorist proposal submitted to Congress by the president in January 2002. In fact, about $3.5 billion of that figure is earmarked for the nation's 36,000 local jurisdictions to spend on planning, equipment, and training. This program would be administered by the Federal Emergency Management Agency and would be distributed based on population size.

Three-letter solution: VPN

In terms of how this communications network of local public safety agencies would work, we believe the answer is simplicity itself and can be summarized in three letters: VPN, or virtual private network. Using that most ubiquitous and useful addition to our communications options—the Internet—VPNs represent a relatively inexpensive but extremely effective way to satisfy Ridge's mandate for municipalities to share information.

A VPN operates like intranet, local area network (LAN), and wide area network (WAN) systems that many companies in private industry currently use to transmit data from one office to another in the same building or across the country. The difference is that VPNs don't require expensive dedicated phone lines and other sophisticated equipment used in other systems. Rather, they use the Internet's structure to send data "wrapped up" in special encrypted packages. Requiring little more than inexpensive routers that "sit" between their networks and the Internet, participating departments can send and receive valuable information to one another quickly and easily.

For example, the suspicious Hempstead police officer described in our example above could query a central data repository and could receive responses indicating that incident reports about a person fitting this individual's description have been filed with several adjacent departments. Armed with this information, the officer can then decide on a specific course of action, which might include continued observation, questioning, or even arrest.

Advantages of VPN

The VPN system offers clear advantages over other communications networks. In addition to its relatively low cost, the system is easy to install, and can link local agencies with the use of a simple dedicated router via API (application program interface) software. In addition, the system can be made relatively secure from outside tampering. But most important is its ability to shift many aspects of community policing from a reactive to a proactive mode.

How can it do this? In addition to providing local police departments with an expanded database, including information on both criminal and noncriminal activities, the system can "flag" potentially controversial activities that require investigation. For example, the system may link seemingly innocent individuals by descriptions, vehicle records, or other data in relationships that hitherto would have been difficult, if not impossible, to detect.

Interactive communication

The ramifications of this kind of "interactive communication" are clear and manifold. By eliminating hours of painstaking investigation by teams of officers, this type of system requires a commitment of far less personnel resources in order to be successful, and can react virtually instantly in almost every situation. Equally important, the expanded database of critical information affords a much greater degree of protection for our officers.

Armed with significant background data about a person, residence, or vehicle, first responders are able to consider expanded approach options. In addition, they will make their approaches with a heightened level of alert when responding to a call. Again, this is police work taking a much more proactive approach to situations that previously were handled much more reactively.

Cost of delay is too high

What has become painfully clear to police department administrators across the country is that the cost of delaying the implementation of this sort of information-sharing network is simply too high in terms of the potential loss of life and property.

Consequently, we are calling on the leaders of our profession to promote the concept of greater sharing of data in their respective regions and to enlist the support of those departments that are technologically prepared to create such a network. We urge them to find qualified technology companies that can help link these departments using VPNs or other systems, and to submit proposals for accomplishing this work, including cost estimates. We believe an efficient VPN can be created at a cost of between $10,000 and $15,000 per department, including necessary software and hardware, if participating agencies currently have some sort of computer record-keeping system in place.

The final step is to petition the federal government, either directly or through state professional associations, for funding to create the system. In the prevailing national climate, such funding should not be difficult to justify or obtain.

We are encouraged by the lead taken by the many farsighted localities and states that have already established shared networks, and by the federal government's efforts to increase the degree of communication and information sharing at the local level. Consequently, we look forward to a future in the United States of America in which public safety and security will be significantly enhanced, thanks in large measure to the wider application of digital technology in the profession of law enforcement.

6 Community threat assessment: A model for police

Bill Flynt and Ron Olin

The war against terrorism has been fought for decades in many battles and with a variety of strategies. While there is a history of domestic and international terrorist activities in the United States, the most deadly attacks had been in foreign locations where American interests and citizens were targets. High profile incidents such as the first World Trade Center attack in 1993 and the Oklahoma City bombing in 1995 prompted discussions of the future of terrorism and the threat of terrorists using weapons of mass effect (WME). These discussions, unfortunately, did not lead to changes in the planning or operations of the majority of law enforcement agencies in the United States.

The United States prepared for, and was more frightened of, the threats surrounding the changeover from the year 1999 to 2000 (Y2K). National leaders agreed that that careful planning and an extraordinary response were necessary to prepare for this transition. Nothing disastrous happened, and we returned to our routines determined not to overreact to future warnings of potential dangers. On September 11, 2001, we were shocked from our complacency. The public's fears of additional terrorist attacks, perhaps using biological, chemical, or radiological weapons, have only increased the perceptions of vulnerability, demands for protection, and questionable assurances that all levels of government are cooperating and responding appropriately.

New antiterrorism role for police executives

The question that is being asked by many law enforcement executives is what is the role of a police chief in antiterrorist response? Police chiefs and other law enforcement executives are viewed by their citizens and elected officials as leaders. During crises, a chief's leadership role broadens to help guide the community through dangerous and turbulent times. Not only careers but also lives depend upon the proper law enforcement response.

Although many senior law enforcement executives are trained in crisis and consequence management, the response to catastrophic terrorism requires new priorities and responsibilities. Some police chiefs have experience in antiterrorism and the terrorist threat; other chiefs have not had the time or opportunity to research topics such as the causes of terrorism, radical fundamentalism, or antiterrorist response. Some police executives are capable of completing threat analyses of their communities, or have staffs trained to prepare such analyses; others have less analytical experience and little or no staff. Many chiefs are simply unprepared for the challenge of countering a world-class terrorist threat in their community. Nonetheless, elected officials and the public expect a police executive and his or her organization to be prepared.

Originally published as "The Red, Gray, and Blue Model: A New Tool to Help Law Enforcement Executives Address the Transformed Security Environment." Reprinted from *The Police Chief*, Vol. LXIX, No. 2, pages 50–59, February, 2002. Copyright held by the International Association of Chiefs of Police, 515 North Washington Street, Alexandria, VA 22314 USA. Further reproduction without express written permission from IACP is strictly prohibited.

Lessons learned from September 11

The terrorist attacks of September 11, 2001, find us all reassessing and redefining our roles as local, state, and federal responders. First, we have realized that we are all potential combatants. Local law enforcement personnel, firefighters, and civilians are participants in the terrorist conflict. Second, all nations are vulnerable. Freedom from fear and particularly the expectations of security by citizens in the United States are the exceptions and not the rule in the world. Third, no single law enforcement agency is capable of a comprehensive antiterrorist response. We must look for solutions inside and outside of our organizations, including the military and other countries, in formulating a more effective terrorist response.

Fourth, the daunting tasks of emergency response, consequence management, and subsequent investigation are the least desirable conclusions to a terrorist event. The goal for all law enforcement agencies must be prevention. Terrorist prevention involves many components but certainly includes comprehensive community threat assessments, new law enforcement training programs, and processes for intelligence gathering. Each of these prevention tools is complex enough to devote a separate article or even a book to the subject. Our purpose in this brief selection is to introduce one model of assessing community threat levels.

The need for an analytical framework

Intelligent thought precedes intelligent action. As we begin to fundamentally reassess our security policies in the aftermath of the September tragedies, we must first look at how we see the new world, and understand what ultimately shapes our perceptions.

Law enforcement executives require a sound analytical framework upon which to base their organization's strategic policies and direct activities to protect communities and their critical infrastructures. Most of the policies and procedures employed by law enforcement, whether recognized explicitly or not, largely focus on countering a specific threat actor (a criminal) or limited universe of threat actors (organized criminals), using relatively static capabilities within a given environment. The framework itself promotes a type of tunnel vision in assessing the security environment. We must expand this analytical framework and view of the world to be capable of including response to state or non-state threat actors (terrorists) employing asymmetric, anonymous, and asynchronous attacks, including the employment of WME.

United States law enforcement organizations at the local and state levels are not traditionally involved in national security operations. Yet, as the events of September 11, 2001, demonstrate, the American public and homeland are vulnerable to attacks that most local law enforcement policies were never designed to counter. In a real sense, local law enforcement is on the front lines of homeland security.

This situation requires local law enforcement to fundamentally reevaluate its perceptions of community threats, the environment in which the agency operates, and police officers' responsibilities and training. Many existing law enforcement policies are inadequate in the current security environment, and the mission of community policing is changing. These events and other developments require a comprehensive re-examination of how law enforcement protects and serves its community.

The challenge at the local level

Let us take as an example the principal focus of an imaginary law enforcement agency whose primary activities are the protection of the population from burglary, the enforcement of traffic laws, and the interdiction of drugs. This focus is driven by the police chief's perception of the criminal threat to citizens and the political environment in the jurisdiction.

The police chief directs the development of his or her organization's major policies towards burglary, traffic, and drug investigation and organizes the agency's capabilities to pursue these goals. Three factors—threat, environment, and individual officer behaviors—are interdependent and interactive. If the police chief's analytical framework does not rigorously and consciously evaluate all three of these elements and their impact on the organization as part of the equation, the overall results for the community may be misdirected. If the police chief fails to recognize a change in the community's threat or environment, the city may be exposed.

Today, we must try to evaluate locally the potential for terrorist events in our communities. Change generally occurs only when existing policies are clearly perceived as inadequate in accomplishing the mission, or the mission changes. Today, we find ourselves with a changed mission; we must think differently. First, let us define more clearly the three elements of community threat assessment: threat, environment, and self. The framework is a way to think or visualize the threat we face, the environment within which the threats operate, and the organization's ability to respond.

The red, gray, and blue model

The red, gray, and blue model discussed in detail below is a starting point for organizations that wish to conduct an analysis of their community threat levels and their most fundamental, macro policies, including organizational force design, equipment provision, training, and even recruitment.

In the model, red represents the many threat types that exist. Gray stands for the environment within which the organization conducts its mission. In Figure 6-1, security policies "balance" at the Venn diagram overlap, shown by the equilateral triangle in the center. "Unbalanced" policies are those that fail to recognize the interdependent and interactive nature of the model's three components. Crafting effective security policies requires understanding and balancing all three elements.

A policy that addresses a threat or a portion of the red circle that does not pertain to or overlap the blue circle is a policy that cannot be implemented by the organization. A policy that can be implemented by an individual or organization (blue) but does not pertain to a threat (red) does not counter a threat. A real world example might be an organization that adopts a policy calling for a computer crime unit (addressing a threat) without possessing the computer resources or police officers trained to implement the policy. Adopting and implementing a policy because an organization can do so does not necessarily counter a threat. Identifying a threat without implementing the appropriate response is also a formula for failure.

Figure 6-1.
The community threat assessment model: Threat, environment, and self.

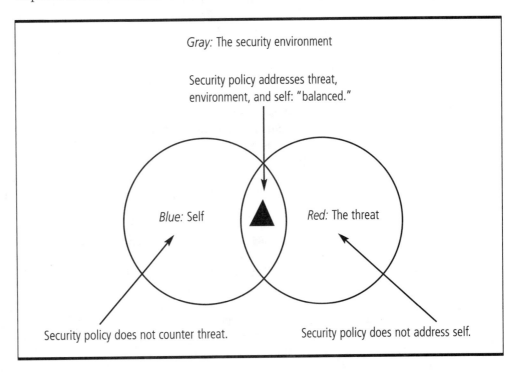

Gray: The security environment

Security policy addresses threat, environment, and self: "balanced."

Blue: Self

Red: The threat

Security policy does not counter threat.

Security policy does not address self.

The threat: red

Identifying threats has become more difficult. The question is what threat?

Assessing capability and intent Threats may be identified by a threat's capability and/or a threat's intent. Attempting to identify threats based on capabilities has lost some measure of importance because so many individuals and groups potentially possess the means to attack a community with super-lethal means. Trying to track capabilities is nearly futile in an environment where capabilities are both easily concealed and proliferating rapidly as the result of technology. Technology provides even small groups with communications and weapons that in the past were held only by national powers.

Technology and the proliferation of knowledge have made biological, radiological, chemical, cyber, and potentially even nuclear capabilities available to non-state actors. Terrorists, as the September 2001 terrorist attacks incontrovertibly show, can use seemingly benign means, such as aircraft and buildings, against a backdrop of a permissive environment, where they accessed flight training and boarded commercial airliners to attack. This observation makes assessing a potential threat's intent much more important. In analyzing a community's threat, we must identify targets, events, and activities that might indicate a potentially desirable intent for a terrorist attack.

In today's increasingly complex security environment, states are not the only major threat actors. The universe of threat actors that law enforcement must contend with has increased dramatically. These may include "lone wolves," foreign intelligence organizations, state-sponsored terrorist groups, ethnic or crime-specific families and cartels, apocalyptic cults, and a host of other nontraditional threat actors.

Investigating a cult Let us take as an example a police agency investigating a cult as a potential threat. A cult may be violent and pose an asymmetric threat to a community. A cult may be a closed, potentially transnational group defined by internal beliefs and purpose. It may even reject mainstream societal norms. A cult leader's control over his followers can exceed that of highly disciplined terrorist organizations or elite military units. Cult leadership can dictate every aspect of a member's life, including schedule, diet, religious beliefs, activities, sex, marriage, child bearing and rearing, dress, education, and, ultimately, thoughts. Gaining acceptance within the cult requires increasing internalization of cult beliefs and norms; the recruit becomes an initiate, a member, and then a trusted operator. Progression between the stages depends on demonstrated behavior under invasive supervision.

Law enforcement's investigation of a criminal cult is difficult because the informer must enter the cult as a recruit and gain access to information within the inner circle. Obtaining access to critical information may take years. Any moderately sophisticated cult aware of surveillance techniques can defeat information-gathering efforts or manipulate perceptions to deceive outsiders. In open societies a large cult can escape attention by even close neighbors.

A violent cult may employ unconventional means and weapons. The anthrax attacks in 2001 against members of the U.S. Senate and others using the U.S. Postal Service are not the first use of biological agents in the United States. In fact, a biological attack involving a cult predates it by some 17 years; the September-October 1984 poisoning of residents in Oregon by disciples of Bhagwan Shree Rajneesh.

In the Rajneesh cult's operation, the leader's intent was strictly political. The cult wished to minimize voter turnout and gain advantage in a local election it viewed as critical to its interests. Devout cultists spread salmonella typhimurium bacteria in 10 local restaurants, resulting in two different waves of outbreaks. The scale of the attack was significant; 751 persons were infected. Contaminated food items differed among the restaurants, and the investigation did not identify a common factor, such as a single food distributor or water supply shared by the restaurants. Operating from a fixed framework of threat, environment, and self, law enforcement at first did not consider the possibility of deliberate contamination. Investigators were trapped within their preconceived analytical framework, and could not critically assess the possibilities.

Identifying and evaluating threats   To simplify the assessment effort, we must identify in each of our communities those known threat actors so as to study and to better understand other potential threats. Generally understanding one threat enables better understanding of other similar threats in their motives, means, methods, and missions. Each threat may be unique in its means, ends, and danger posed. However, failure to conduct analyses of different threats in our jurisdictions is inexcusable given the open-source intelligence resources available even to small, local law enforcement organizations.

In evaluating the terrorist threat, a concern is often expressed that local or state law enforcement is ill informed of information known to federal agencies. Yet, the best information on local activities is usually found in the notebooks, interactions, and memories of the local law enforcement officer. Many times, the protocol for reporting, analyzing, and using intelligence information is the critical obstacle to success. When law enforcement agencies learn to view threat, environment, and self and create procedures to share their knowledge, communities will be safer. From a security perspective we want to know who are the threats, their means of attack, their targets, and the goals they are pursuing.

The environment: gray

Typically, law enforcement organizations do a poor job of objectively assessing themselves—their political and security environments. Politics, bureaucratic inertia, a seemingly insurmountable workload, and the statistically insignificant number of actual terrorist events create an atmosphere of futility and complacency for the average law enforcement executive. Assessment of the community environment is difficult, but necessary. Police chiefs can use the information obtained in evaluating the security environment to transform their organizations into agencies focused on prevention and primed for response.

Police chiefs and law enforcement executives think they know the environment in which their organizations operate. The environment influences both potential threat and law enforcement response and can be modeled using core assumptions about community characteristics. For example, a model of a law enforcement organization's security environment would include information about the presence of critical infrastructure in the jurisdiction. These critical infrastructure targets may be easily accessible and vulnerable to sabotage. In the past, we have viewed critical infrastructure as resources not targets.

The new mindset must be to view one's community as a target. A police chief cannot really know his or her own environment until one looks at it as a terrorist would. In completing the assessment there are resources available that we rarely access. Expert help may be obtained from governmental, corporate, and community resources. If a police chief takes the time to complete the assessment, it is possible to build a critical objective perspective about the threats a jurisdiction may face.

Self: blue

Understanding self means the way of viewing the role of the police chief, law enforcement executive, or individual police officer in responding to the new terrorist challenge. We must now clearly evaluate our capabilities, available resources, courses of action, and desired outcomes. Part of the assessment involves understanding the potential for change and adaptation the organization must exercise in transforming itself to meet the challenges posed by the current terrorist threat. Resources are finite, and policy development must recognize this constraint by prioritizing prevention and response.

We have already noted the importance of enlightened policies to guide law enforcement agencies. Another example of organizational policy that reinforces these perceptions over time is the specific course of training received by officers. Training must focus on the new duties perceived to be most relevant to the officer in accomplishing the organization's mission. Antiterrorism must become part of this mission.

Officers must also be given the intellectual tools to counter anticipated threats occurring within their own environment. This formal social indoctrination, in turn, reinforces future behavior. When we rely exclusively on our existing framework of perceptions, and as a police officer becomes the veteran officer contributing to the training of new recruits, we inevitably fall into the "we've always done it that way" school of thought that views the status quo as something sacred to defend. Our actions and omissions of actions will define future terrorist opportunities.

Looking ahead

The red, gray, and blue framework is an intellectual tool that may help law enforcement executives in thinking about the changed security environment. It can assist police chiefs and law enforcement executives as a point of clarification in the analysis of their policies, and help law enforcement avoid becoming prisoners of an irrelevant intellectual framework. Until we critically examine our conventional wisdom about the threats we face, the environment in which we operate, and even our own cultural characteristics and predisposition, we risk missing important signals and may fail to anticipate and prevent the next terrorist threat.

The future for law enforcement response to the terrorist threat must be prevention and a new mind-set for law enforcement officers. What was not traditionally a law enforcement priority, terrorism, has become a local concern. Police chiefs and police officers must consider themselves agents of national security. They need to refocus on their communities and law enforcement interactions within them for both crime fighting and terrorism prevention roles. Law enforcement executives should look for ways to improve their professionalism, training, and intelligence gathering capabilities while recognizing the increasing importance of interagency cooperation.

The current world threat demands that law enforcement executives recognize and respond to the new challenges that have been presented to them. This task will require new tools and approaches. We must reach a national consensus in much the same way we did for Y2K preparations to commit our law enforcement resources, training, intelligence, analysis, and prevention skills in addressing the terrorist threats of the 21st century. Only with such sustained efforts will we preserve our safety and security.

The views contained in this selection are those of the authors—Bill Flynt, a lieutenant colonel in the U.S. Army, and Ron Olin, the chief of police in Lawrence, Kansas—and do not purport to reflect the position of the U.S. Department of the Army; the Department of Defense; the Lawrence, Kansas, Police Department; or any other government office or agency.

7 Preventing terrorist acts: A new challenge for law enforcement

D. Douglas Bodrero

Since the tragic attacks of September 11, 2001, state and local law enforcement administrators from agencies of all sizes have asked a similar question: "What is the role of state and local law enforcement in a post-September 11 environment?"

From the federal standpoint, President Bush created the White House Office of Homeland Security. U.S. Attorney General John Ashcroft has testified before Congress that "the fight against terrorism is now the first and overriding priority of the Department of Justice."[1] Federal Bureau of Investigation (FBI) Director Robert Mueller has, with the approval of Congress, reorganized the FBI to increase emphasis on counterterrorism, counterintelligence, cybercrime, and relations with state and local law enforcement.[2] Congress has taken testimony from a broad spectrum of experts seeking advice on how to better protect our citizens in a new age of increased terrorism threats.

Several governors have created state homeland security offices, all trying to determine how to best protect the lives and property of American citizens. While debates have gone on at the national level..., state and local law enforcement leaders have met with their associations and neighboring chiefs and sheriffs as well as entered into dialogue with senior administrative staff.

The role of state and local law enforcement

During this period of change, one thing is likely to remain the same. State and local law enforcement's role in tomorrow's world will be the same as it has always been: to protect the lives and property of citizens. While some states have mobilized National Guard troops, the primary source of protection of America's communities remains the thin blue line provided by America's law enforcement community. Unless there are additional catastrophic attacks, it is doubtful that federal military troops will be patrolling the cities and counties of America. State and local law enforcement agencies will be performing the job they have traditionally performed, only in a drastically altered environment.

The primary goal of law enforcement has been, and remains, to ensure public safety. The renewed threat of terrorism has spread fear and apprehension to Americans of all social and economic classes. This renewed fear and concern have changed, and will continue to change, the environment in which all law enforcement activities are conducted.

The rise in domestic terrorism

Since the Oklahoma City attacks in 1995 and a subsequent increase in incidents of terrorism by special-interest groups, state and local law enforcement has been concerned about the increase in domestic-inspired terrorism. Before September 11, 2001, attacks on American interests had occurred overseas (with the exception of the 1993 World Trade Center bombing in New York City), and state and local law enforcement saw international counterterrorism as a responsibility of the federal law enforcement and intelligence agencies. As noted historian Thomas C. Schelling has written, "Surprise, when it happens to a government, is likely to be a complicated, diffused, bureaucratic thing. It includes neglect of responsibility but also responsibility so poorly defined or so ambiguously delegated that action gets lost...It includes the contingencies that occur to no one, but also those that everyone assumes someone else has taken care of."[3]

Given the tragic events of September 11, actions concerning the planning or execution of terrorist acts on U.S. soil are the concern of every law enforcement agency, regardless of size or area of responsibility. Every terrorist event, every act of planning and preparation for that event (if conducted inside the United States) occurs in some local law enforcement agency's jurisdiction. No agency is closer to the activities within its community than the law enforcement agency that has responsibility and jurisdiction for protecting that community.

A new focus on WMD

After the Oklahoma City bombing, state and local law enforcement directed a significant amount of effort at improving America's ability to respond to terrorist acts, particularly incidents involving the use or potential use of weapons of mass destruction (WMD). In testimony before the House Subcommittee on Terrorism and Homeland Security on September 26, 2001, Bruce Hoffman of the Rand Corporation said, "The focus of U.S. counterterrorism policy in recent years has arguably been too weighted towards the 'high end' threats from biological and chemical weapons and was based mainly on planning for extreme worst-case scenarios."[4] Fuel-laden airliners were used as weapons of mass destruction, but they were not factored into typical, if any, WMD scenarios.

Traditional counterterrorism planning involves a three-prong approach: interdiction and prevention, crisis management, and consequence management. While no one would question the need for increased first responder training, it has now become evident that law enforcement also needs to concentrate efforts on investigating, detecting, and preventing acts of terrorism.

Prevention as first priority

In a November 8, 2001, speech announcing a reorganization of federal law enforcement resources, Attorney General Ashcroft stated, "Today the American people call upon the Federal Bureau of Investigation to put prevention of terrorism at the center of its law enforcement and national security efforts."[5] The executive summary of the report from the National Commission on Terrorism states, "Priority one is to prevent terrorist attacks. U.S. intelligence and law enforcement communities must use the full scope of their authority to collect intelligence regarding terrorist plans and methods."[6]

As state and local law enforcement carry out their traditional roles in the new war on terrorism, they also must assume a greater responsibility in the area of interdiction and prevention of terrorist acts. After all, who knows the community and its citizens better than the cop on the beat, the deputy on patrol, or the trooper covering his usual assignment?

Four critical steps

Four critical steps are necessary in order to be more effective in interdiction and prevention efforts. First, through training, we need to better understand the enemy. Second, a comprehensive counterterrorism planning process needs to be initiated. Third, we need to increase and enhance intelligence gathering and analytical capabilities. Last, we need to work cooperatively at all government levels in the formation of, or the participation in, terrorism task forces and/or working groups.

Training as a means to understanding

In *The Art of War*, military strategist Sun Tzu wrote, "If you know the enemy and know yourself, you need not fear the results of a hundred battles. If you know yourself and not the enemy, for every victory gained you will also suffer a defeat. If you know neither yourself or the enemy, you will succumb in every battle."[7]

Typical criminals or terrorists?   State and local law enforcement officers are experienced in dealing with the "typical criminal." Most individuals with whom law enforcement comes in contact are driven by greed and/or control issues. Terrorists, on the other hand, operate on completely different agendas unfamiliar to most law enforcement investigators. Consider the following examples:

- Where typical criminals are opportunistic, extremists are focused. Targets are selected for a particular purpose, as is the method of attack.
- Where typical criminals are uncommitted, terrorictc are extremely committed. The events of September 11 demonstrated that up to 19 individuals were willing to sacrifice their lives to carry out the attacks.
- Typical criminals are often self-centered, while extremists, generally, are team-oriented, operate in cells, and often are unaware of the activities or existence of other cells within the same organization.
- Typical criminals are undisciplined and may be deterred by potential consequences. Extremists, on the other hand, are often highly disciplined and will continue to carry out their attacks even when apprehension and/or personal danger are imminent.
- Typical criminals are untrained, while recent events have demonstrated that terrorists are often highly trained.
- Typical criminals are escape-oriented, whereas criminal extremists are attack-oriented and will often target their pursuers.

Methods and ideologies   Obviously, additional comparisons could be offered; however, it should be evident that in order to understand and effectively interdict terrorist-motivated individuals, law enforcement must first understand their methods as well as ideologies.

Many extremists adhere to nontraditional religious beliefs, which serve as a foundation and motivation for their actions. Theology does not precipitate terrorist behavior, but it does sometimes provide an atmosphere that justifies an attack on traditional social structures. A more thorough examination of extremist ideologies is necessary to better understand how to detect and deter extremist-related attacks.

It is therefore important that the first step in enhancing state and local agencies' ability to effectively deter terrorism involves a segment of training to better understand extremist behavior. Additionally, effective training can also arm an officer with the tools needed to conduct a successful investigation. Up to now, training opportunities have been limited or concentrated on a particular ideology or terrorist group. In the post-September 11 environment, it will be necessary for all law enforcement personnel, especially investigators assigned to terrorism-related activities, to avail themselves of training opportunities that may help them better understand their enemy in the war on terrorism.

Counterterrorism planning

The next step in confronting the terrorism threat at a state and local level involves the implementation of an effective planning process. At first glance, the scope and methodologies involved in addressing the terrorism issue may appear overwhelming. State and local law enforcement administrators have demonstrated effectiveness in planning for extraordinary events, and most have established good working relationships with other participants in the planning process. By creating a specific counterterrorism planning process, administrators can better respond to a terrorist incident and also be in a favorable position to identify and prevent an incident from occurring.

Leading from the Front: Law Enforcement's Role in Combating and Preparing for Domestic Terrorism, published by the International Association of Chiefs of Police (IACP), provides a valuable outline that should be followed in initiating an effective planning process.[8] Readers are encouraged to review that report for suggestions and direction as it relates to effective counterterrorism planning.

Intelligence gathering and analysis

Since the attacks of September 11, the role of terrorism-related intelligence has received considerable attention from the media, policy makers, and the public. No one questions that a law enforcement agency's approach to terrorist and/or extremist threats should be based on effective intelligence. The report from the National Commission on Terrorism states, "Good intelligence is the best weapon against international terrorism. Obtaining information about the identity, goals, plans, and vulnerabilities of terrorists is extremely difficult. Yet, no other single policy effort is more important for preventing, preempting, and responding to attacks."[9] While the report specifically addresses international terrorism, the same rule applies for terrorism in general.

Lawrence B. Sulc, in his book *Law Enforcement Counter Intelligence*, writes, "Law enforcement—the 'thin blue line'—is the first line of defense. It is often the last line of defense, as well."[10] The general mission of law enforcement intelligence is the gathering of information about individuals and groups who may pose a threat and the use of that knowledge to forecast future activities.[11] In addition to obtaining timely intelligence information, law enforcement also needs the resources and capabilities to use that information in a prompt fashion. Law enforcement must collect information and process that information into an understandable format that allows it to be prioritized and disseminated.

Useful resources   While not all agencies are able to staff full-time criminal intelligence units, there are a number of resources available to agencies to assist with intelligence gathering and analysis. The Regional Information Sharing Systems (RISS) program is an intelligence-sharing network that has a goal of assisting state and local criminal justice agencies. The network is controlled by its members: local, state, and federal agencies. Since September 11, the six RISS centers have expanded their strategies to assist state and local law enforcement in the terrorist intelligence field. RISS information sharing occurs electronically through a bulletin board (RISSLeads), live chat sessions, a conferencing capability, and pointer indices. In addition, RISS maintains a secure intranet for electronic networking throughout the United States (for further information on RISS, see the web site at www.iir.com/riss).

Other regional databases include those of the High Intensity Drug Trafficking Areas (HIDTAs). While the primary HIDTA mission is reducing drug trafficking, most HIDTAs have resources useful in other intelligence gathering and analysis activities.

Another resource is the El Paso Intelligence Center (EPIC). EPIC is a cooperative effort staffed by personnel from 15 federal law enforcement agencies and has entered into information-sharing agreements with law enforcement agencies from all 50 states (for further information, visit EPIC's web site at www.usdoj.gov/dea/programs/epic.htm).

In addition, most states have a designated Interpol representative who can assist in obtaining information or in facilitating information exchange involving international criminal cases. Another resource is the International Association of Law Enforcement Intelligence Analysts (IALEIA) (for further information, see its web site at www.ialeia.org). In addition, several states maintain state-based intelligence systems that may also be used.

Obviously, much more could be written concerning the need for an effective intelligence gathering and analytical process. Suffice it to say that in this new post-September 11 environment, every agency needs to reevaluate its intelligence process, formulate partnerships with other organizations, and avail itself of opportunities for additional training and networking to obtain the information necessary to protect its community.

Threat assessments   Another area of concern is the use of intelligence to produce threat assessments. Such assessments are useful in evaluating characteristics of extremist groups that may be operational within particular jurisdictions, analyzing risks, and measuring violence potential. Effective threat assessments can be useful for tactical and strategic purposes to target and neutralize extremist groups before they have an opportunity to commit acts of violence. A threat assessment is a combination of gathering information through the intelligence process, analyzing risks that may be present, evaluating the characteristics of an extremist organization, and formulating an assessment that can be used in identifying initiatives that may be necessary to disrupt extremist-related activities.[12]

Terrorism task forces and working groups

Obtaining good intelligence and using that intelligence in a strategic application to disrupt criminal extremist activities is critical. Useful though it may be, the question that has plagued law enforcement at all levels since September 11 has been how to best share critical intelligence information between agencies and organizations. In November 2001, Attorney General Ashcroft said, "Our partners in state and local law enforcement have been our eyes and ears and muscle on the ground...We must develop a seamless relationship with state and local law enforcement agencies." He further stated, "We must have information technology from this decade, not from several generations ago, so that we can share intelligence and have the interoperability that a coordinated response to terrorism demands."[13]

During the 108th Annual IACP Conference in Toronto in October 2001, law enforcement administrators nationwide expressed concern to FBI Director Mueller that a better method of sharing intelligence information between organizations was necessary. Police administrators were frustrated at the issuance of national alerts by federal officials without the accompanying information to allow those administrators to effectively evaluate the risk and direct their resources to effectively address the risk. An article that appeared in the November 12, 2001, issue of *Time*, titled "Measuring the Threat," outlines some issues on both sides of the argument surrounding intelligence information dissemination.[14]

FBI Director Mueller has committed to improving the flow of information between the FBI and state and local law enforcement agencies and, in return, state and local agencies need to be patient as this process is redefined and improved. Agencies at all levels need to also reexamine their information sharing policies and practices and discuss within their associations, organizations, and agencies methods to facilitate a better exchange of information at all levels.

Without question this is an ongoing process; however, it is hoped that in the new environment, significant progress will be made.

It has become evident that terrorism is an issue that no single agency, no single organization, and no single unit of government can address in a vacuum. The creation of the White House Office of Homeland Security at the national level, with similar agency redefinition in many states, demonstrates that to adequately and effectively address this issue a cooperative cross-jurisdictional approach is necessary. The FBI's creation of joint terrorism task forces has proven to be an effective method of addressing the terrorism threat, while providing a means for the pooling of resources and the sharing of information with state and local agencies.

In addition, after the September attacks, Attorney General Ashcroft directed every U.S. attorney to establish an antiterrorism task force to coordinate the dissemination of information and to assist in the development of an investigative and prosecutive strategy.

However, it is important that the newly created task forces work cooperatively with state and local law enforcement and not simply create another level of bureaucracy. If no formal terrorism task force exists in a particular jurisdiction, local law enforcement administrators can create a terrorism working group to facilitate coordination, cooperation, and information exchange.

Conclusion

State and local law enforcement agencies have been, and always will be, the first line of defense in the protection of life and property within their communities. With the increased emphasis on defending the United States as a result of the September attacks, law enforcement's traditional role to "serve and protect" will be a carried out in the future in a new environment. The heroism demonstrated in New York, Washington, D.C., and Pennsylvania has once again demonstrated to the world that America's people and law enforcement are ready, willing, and able to meet any challenges or threats and respond to any crisis that may occur within their communities.

Notes

[1] Brian Friel, "Justice Department Streamlines, Reorganizes to Focus on Terrorism," *GovExec.com*, November 8, 2001; January 10, 2002, http://www.govexec.com/dailyfed/1101/110801b1.htm.

[2] U.S. Department of Justice, Federal Bureau of Investigation, press release, Washington, D.C., December 3, 2001; Federal Bureau of Investigation web site, January 10, 2002, http://www.fbi.gov/pressrel/pressrel01/reorg120301.htm.

[3] Thomas C. Schelling, foreword, *Pearl Harbor: Warning and Decision,* by Roberta Wohlstetter (Palo Alto, Calif.: Stanford University Press, 1962), quoted in National Commission on Terrorism, *Countering the Changing Threat of International Terrorism* (Washington, D.C.: U.S. Government Printing Office, 2000); Federation of American Scientists web site, January 10, 2002, http://www.fas.org/irp/threat/commission.html.

[4] Bruce Hoffman, "Re-thinking Terrorism in Light of a War on Terrorism," testimony before the Subcommittee on Terrorism and Homeland Security, House Permanent Select Committee on Intelligence, U.S. House of Representatives, September 26, 2001; Rand Corporation web site, January 10, 2002, http://www.rand.org/publications/ct/ct182/ct182.pdf.

[5] U.S. Department of Justice, "Attorney General Ashcroft and Deputy Attorney General Thompson Announce Reorganization and Mobilization of the Nation's Justice and Law Enforcement Resources," transcript of a speech delivered in Washington, D.C., November 8, 2001; U.S. Department of Justice web site, January 10, 2002, www.usdoj.gov/ag/speeches/2001/agresisremarks11_08.htm.

[6] National Commission on Terrorism, executive summary, *Countering the Changing Threat of International Terrorism* (Washington, D.C.: U.S. Government Printing Office, 2000), iv; Federation of American Scientists web site, January 10, 2002, http://www.fas.org/irp/threat/commission.html.

[7] Sun Tzu, *The Art of War* (New York: Oxford University Press, 1984).

[8] International Association of Chiefs of Police, *Leading from the Front: Law Enforcement's Role in Combating and Preparing for Domestic Terrorism* (Alexandria, Va.: IACP, 2001); International Association of Chiefs of Police web site, January 10, 2002, http://www.theiacp.org/documents/pdfs/terrorism.pdf.

[9] National Commission on Terrorism, *Countering the Changing Threat of International Terrorism*, 7.

[10] Lawrence B. Sulc, *Law Enforcement Counterintelligence* (Shawnee Mission, Kan.: Varro Press, 1996), xiii.

[11] International Association of Law Enforcement Intelligence Analysts and Law Enforcement Intelligence Unit, *Intelligence 2000: Revising the Basic Elements* (Lawrenceville, N.J.: IALEIA, 2000), 7.

[12] California Department of Justice, *Threat Assessments: A Guide to Evaluating and Analyzing Criminal Extremist Groups*, by Jerry Marynik (Sacramento, Calif.: California Department of Justice, 1997).

[13] U.S. Department of Justice, "Attorney General Ashcroft and Deputy Attorney General Thompson Announce Reorganization."

[14] Daniel Eisenberg, "Measuring the Threat," *Time*, November 12, 2001, 34.

8 | Traffic law enforcement and homeland security

Jeffrey W. Runge

Since September 11, 2001, the United States has made unprecedented efforts to ensure the security of all Americans. State and local governments have joined forces with the federal government and private industry to redefine policies and enact laws that will help protect our way of life.

The U.S. Department of Transportation's National Highway Traffic Safety Administration (NHTSA) has been working to develop strategies, training, and resources to help law enforcement agencies. Our efforts are crafted to complement existing initiatives that safeguard our nation from security threats. The law enforcement community has always been one of NHTSA's steadfast and visible partners in traffic safety. Enforcement of traffic safety laws is crucial to the mission of reducing deaths and injuries on our highways. This includes enforcement of seat belt and child safety seat and impaired driving laws as well as addressing the problems caused by motorists who willfully violate posted speed limits. Not to be overlooked is the attention law enforcement gives the problem of reckless or aggressive driving behaviors that threaten the public safety. NHTSA studies have shown that high-visibility enforcement efforts combined with innovative public education initiatives can reduce the number of crash-related deaths and injuries.

Benefits beyond the traffic stop

I am pleased that law enforcement officers recognize that traffic law enforcement benefits can go far beyond the traffic stop. When suspicious behavior is observed and heightened awareness is employed, it is possible to reduce crime in the community as well as illegal activities that could lead to terrorism or other violent crimes. In many cases, officers conducting routine traffic enforcement have apprehended fugitives. Officers at traffic stops have seized stolen vehicles and merchandise, and uncovered evidence of child abuse. Alert officers have identified vehicles carrying explosives and hazardous materials. Routine traffic stops have resulted in law enforcement agencies gathering intelligence on a wide range of issues associated with criminal activity.

We all remember that terrorist Timothy McVeigh was identified in a traffic stop because Trooper Charlie Hangar of the Oklahoma Highway Patrol noticed a license plate violation. McVeigh was subsequently convicted and executed for his role in the bombing of the Alfred P. Murrah building in Oklahoma City on April 19, 1995.

Another example of the value of traffic stops is drug interdiction. The Drug Enforcement Administration (DEA) estimates that 40 percent of all drug arrests in this country are the outgrowth of traffic stops.

Originally published as "The Role of Traffic Law Enforcement in Homeland Security." Reprinted from *The Police Chief*, Vol. LXIX, No. 10, pages 90–98, October, 2002. Copyright held by the International Association of Chiefs of Police, 515 North Washington Street, Alexandria, VA 22314 USA. Further reproduction without express written permission from IACP is strictly prohibited.

"Click It or Ticket" campaign

During a 14-day Click It or Ticket safety belt traffic law enforcement campaign in NHTSA's region 4 (Alabama, Florida, Georgia, Kentucky, Mississippi, North Carolina, South Carolina, and Tennessee) in May 2001, officers apprehended 1,471 fugitives, recovered 254 stolen vehicles, and identified a variety of other criminal violations while writing citations for seatbelt violations.[1]

Before September 11, 2001, routine efforts by traffic law enforcement officers had already helped to identify some terrorists who were later determined to have been involved in the attacks:

- On September 9, 2001, a Maryland State Police Trooper stopped Aiad S. Jarrah for speeding. He was the terrorist who later flew the American Airlines plane into the World Trade Center.[2]

- On April 1, 2001, an Oklahoma State Trooper stopped Nawaf Alhazmi, who is believed to have helped hijack American Airlines flight 77 and crash it into the Pentagon, for speeding and not wearing a safety belt. Following the terrorist attack, his car was found at Dulles International Airport outside Washington, D.C. The information obtained at the traffic stop and from the National Criminal Information Center (NCIC) was critical in helping the FBI trace Alhazmi back to the Oklahoma traffic stop and determine how the terrorist attack was planned.[3]

While these stops did not prevent the terrorist acts against our country, they show that traffic law enforcement can play a crucial role in helping identify and apprehend criminals who threaten Americans' security. To this end, NHTSA has been working diligently to develop training, strategies, and resources that will help law enforcement agencies train their personnel to more effectively understand their critical role in traffic enforcement. This training will better prepare officers to recognize suspicious activities.

Traffic enforcement and criminal interdiction

The U.S. Department of Justice and NHTSA have collaborated to provide training to state and local law enforcement academy personnel to teach patrol officers about the critical relationship between traffic enforcement and criminal enforcement. The course, Conducting Complete Traffic Stops: A Crash and Crime Reduction Effort, discusses how law enforcement officers can effectively, legally, and professionally conduct criminal interdiction at traffic stops when suspicious indicators are present. Specifically, it covers such topics as the following:

- The relationship between traffic enforcement and criminal interdiction at the traffic stop
- Suspicious physical indicators
- Interview techniques to gain more information about the immediate criminal activity but also to gather additional intelligence about other matters
- Legal issues
- Concealment locations
- Professionalism at the stop.

NHTSA training

NHTSA continues to train academy and law enforcement agency instructors to conduct this course and to make the curriculum available throughout the country. Law enforcement agencies need only to contact one of NHTSA's regional offices to set up a course in your area.

NHTSA has made certain that this traffic enforcement training program is conducted in full compliance with constitutional and statutory safeguards that have been established to preserve the rights of citizens, the prescriptions of case law, and the sanctioned policies and practices of law enforcement agencies. By following proper procedures, the rights of innocent drivers and passengers will be protected and, at the same time, the rights and procedures will be in place for legal and ethical prosecutions.

Enforcement issues related to terrorism

During this uncertain time of rebuilding and strengthening our communities, there are a number of issues relevant to traffic law enforcement that will need to be resolved with the help of our federal, state, and local law enforcement partners if we are to be successful in enhancing the safety of the United States and reducing the threat posed by terrorists. These include the following issues:[4]

- Maintaining a high level of traffic law enforcement. Unfortunately, the unexpected demand for personnel to support homeland security issues has created revenue shortages and caused personnel cutbacks in traffic law enforcement. Law enforcement agencies need to consider innovative scheduling techniques that commit a greater percentage of their personnel to traffic enforcement so that these complete traffic stop procedures can be employed. This deployment demonstrates that traffic law enforcement is a vital part of homeland security. As a way of coping with this drain on existing resources, personnel from traffic safety agencies, state legislatures, and federal agencies may need to explore new ways of providing support for traffic law enforcement and patrols that practice these special patrol techniques.

- Real-time access to driver data at the point of the stop for detecting unlicensed, unregistered, and suspended motorists. This is vital for identifying terrorists.

- Encouraging citizens to report suspicious activities on our roadways.

- Encouraging better coordination between emergency medical personnel and law enforcement so when terrorist acts do occur, emergency vehicles can rapidly respond with medical care in a timely manner.

- Continually working with community groups. Since law enforcement officers are already present promoting traffic safety in public places, they are in a good position to work in partnership with citizens to take part in homeland security efforts in their own communities. For example, NHTSA has for many years worked with communities to establish neighborhood WATCH (When All the Citizens Help) programs. Now, since President Bush has called for the creation of the Citizen Corps that encourages the formation of WATCH programs (visit www.usaonwatch.org for more), this is an especially important role for law enforcement officers.[5]

Community policing and homeland security

Law enforcement officers can play a vital role in investigating and preventing future attacks. Patrol operations—and specifically traffic law enforcement—provides a way to track down information related to terrorism. Officers on everyday patrol make stops, respond to calls for service, and perform a variety of community policing activities. If they are properly trained in what to look for and what questions to ask when interacting with citizens, they can be a tremendous source of intelligence for their state and federal homeland security counterparts.[6]

NHTSA continues to promote intelligence-led policing and the exchange of information among law enforcement agencies so that law enforcement officers can perform better at the traffic stop. More effort needs to be put into improving the integration and compatibility of local, state, federal and international criminal justice information systems.[7] Federal agencies including the Drug Enforcement Administration, Federal Bureau of Investigation, Immigration and Naturalization Service, and others are being encouraged to implement a comprehensive data-sharing system that allows traffic law enforcement officers to access information in a timely manner.

Highway safety and the National Driver Register

Between fiscal year 1999 and fiscal year 2002 alone, NHTSA awarded a total of $32 million in Section 411 incentive grants to encourage states to take effective actions to improve the timeliness, accuracy, completeness, uniformity, and accessibility of their highway safety data. In addition, funds were awarded for the National Driver Register, a NHTSA program that facilitates the interstate transfer of driver licensing information concerning problem drivers whose licenses to drive have been suspended or revoked for cause. Next year, NHTSA looks to improve its ability to share data with the states.

When officers find other criminal activity at a traffic stop, they are trained, when appropriate, not to let the issue "die on the side of the road" with a simple arrest because it may have broader implications. For example, if there is suspicious cargo in the trunk that could be terrorism-related, they will use a "controlled delivery," or a sting operation, to apprehend additional criminal elements, often in other jurisdictions. This requires open lines of communication, information sharing, and high levels of cooperation.

Conclusion

NHTSA is aware that training is needed for law enforcement officers to adjust to the changing focus of their operations and to become equipped to apprehend individuals who operate with different motivations, have different objectives, and use much deadlier weapons than traditional criminals.[8] The key to a successful nationwide program is for law enforcement agencies to manage the expectations of the communities or states that they serve. Confidence of the citizens in the appropriateness and effectiveness of proposed strategies and enforcement efforts must be measured. In the long run, the public's realistic expectations will enable law enforcement agencies to perform optimally, and, more importantly, increase the community's sense of security in the face of imminent terrorist threats.

September 11, 2001, has certainly made everyone at NHTSA look at the difficulties in providing the services necessary to make the public feel safe on the nation's streets and highways. We realize that our law enforcement agency partners provide the best protection possible in the face of mounting service challenges and budget pressures. Americans now realize the vital role officers have in carrying out the public trust to provide safety and security. Meeting those challenges will take determination, creativity, and, above all, leadership.

Safety is in the forefront of the nation's consciousness, and it is NHTSA's top priority.

Notes

[1] Troy R. Ayers, regional administrator, NHTSA Region 4 Office, Atlanta, Georgia, telephone interview, April 4, 2002.

[2] Maryland State Police, news release, January 7, 2002.

[3] Oklahoma Department of Public Safety, news release, February 2002.

[4] Earl M. Sweeney, chairman, highway Safety Committee, International Association of Chiefs of Police, letter to Jeffrey W. Runge, M.D., December 4, 2001.

[5] "'USA on Watch' Unveiled," *Sheriff*, March–April 2002, 9–10.

[6] Sweeney, letter to Jeffrey W. Runge, M.D., December 4, 2001.

[7] Gene Voegtlin, "Legislative Alert: IACP Testifies on Local Law Enforcement Role in Homeland Defense," *Police Chief* 69, February 2002, 8.

[8] "'USA on Watch' Unveiled," 9–10.

Part III

Preparedness

9 | Incident responsibility and accountability: Who's in charge?

By Timothy Elliott

No matter what form the next terrorist attack on America takes, count on two questions to arise quickly: "What the hell happened?" and "Who's in charge?"

War stories abound of "who's-in-charge" [debates] devolving into shoving matches: cops vs. fire, locals vs. state, the FBI vs. everybody. Sure, there are plenty of war stories, but how about a success story for a change? One can't look to the initial World Trade Center (WTC) response, certainly.

While never diminishing the courage demonstrated by emergency personnel that day, internal reviews paint an abysmal picture of command, control and communication. A July 7, 2002, report in the *New York Times* distilled the bitter truth: "... [C]lear warnings, captured on police radio tapes, were transmitted 21 minutes before the [second] building fell, and officials say they were relayed to police officers, most of whom managed to escape.

"Yet most firefighters never heard those warnings, or earlier orders to get out. Their radio system failed frequently that morning. Even if the radio network had been reliable, it was not linked to the police system. And the police and fire commanders guiding the rescue efforts did not talk to one another during the crisis."

No incident command system. Separate fire and police command posts. Open animosity (then and now) between fire and police personnel. No wonder the *Times* reporters referred to the dynamic as "tribal feuding."

Maybe that elusive success story lies 230-odd miles south of NYC. Many observers (though not all) now point to the Pentagon response as the very model of how to handle a suspected terrorist attack that is at once incident scene and crime scene.

The Pentagon: A good start

When American Airlines Flight 77 slammed into the west side of the Pentagon on Sept. 11, the Arlington County Fire Department (ACFD) called the ball.

"We had incident command within two minutes of the time the plane hit the Pentagon," says Ed Plaugher, chief of the ACFD. "Our first-arriving unit, as is this department's procedure, established incident command. And we maintained our incident command system for 11 days, until we turned it over to the FBI at 0700 on the 21st."

In effect, a local fire department assumed command of an incident that directly affected multiple communities, two states, the District of Columbia, the Army, Navy, Air Force, and Marines, plus nearly every federal agency in existence. They were all right across the Potomac, too; who would have ever guessed things could be so smooth?

"My fears of an incident in the nation's capital with every federal response unit at our doorstep were not founded at all," Plaugher says. "The federal family, the state family, the volunteer responders, nobody challenged our authority to run this incident using

Originally published as "Who's in Charge Here?" *Homeland Protection Professional*, Vol. 1, No. 1, pages 22–26, July/August, 2002. Published by A. J. Parrino & Associates, Western Springs, Illinois. Reprinted with permission of the publisher.

ICS. We changed it as the circumstances dictated, but we did not deviate from the pure incident command system."

Plaugher notes the near-simultaneous attack in New York City drew its share of federal resources, of course. Still, he attributes the strength of his department's operation to the planning and relationships established before the attack.

The Pentagon: Behind the curtain

So is Arlington County's Pentagon response (ICS, alternating daytime/nighttime incident commanders, multi-jurisdictional command and control) an ideal, adaptable model for others? Adaptable, certainly. Ideal? No, but what system is?

The brigades of federal representatives waving badges at the Pentagon command post didn't materialize because the jurisdictional lines were straightforward, says Garry L. Briese, executive director of the International Association of Fire Chiefs and a long-time advocate for terrorism preparedness.

"It didn't happen because it was a Department of Defense (DOD) facility," Briese says. "It was *the* DOD facility, an anomaly that can't be repeated someplace else." Briese says the commander of the Military District of Washington conferred with Plaugher and told him, "We're here to support you." That's a lot cleaner process than one's likely to find in a civilian environment.

Still, though the federal-versus-local angle worked out fine, there were plenty of woes to suggest that the Pentagon wasn't a flawless command performance.

"As much as we want to paint it, make it look good, the Pentagon response left much to be desired," Briese said. "It was better than it could have been, but it still wasn't what it should have been."

Most of the same operational, command issues that plagued the response to the AirFlorida crash in 1982 appeared September 11, 2001, he said. "The lines were a little cleaner, maybe, because the Pentagon plane didn't crash on the border, but D.C. came over and operated independently," Briese says. "They did not get into the command system. They operated totally independently from Ed Plaugher, took equipment and went back across the river."

"You still had volunteers showing up, abandoning apparatus, not going to staging areas, independent operations. Is that better than 1982? Well, the fire went out. Ed did great and he had a lot of cooperation, but nothing big changed. From an operational standpoint, that's a disappointment."

RPI, a frequently used federal contractor, interviewed hundreds of responders to the Pentagon attack and assembled an after-action report. The first draft reportedly included a warts-and-all assessment of the incident response, including the widely reported dust-up about missing gear.

Arlington firefighters confronted several District of Columbia Fire Department (DCFD) firefighters and accused them of trying to leave the Pentagon scene with more than $30,000 of Arlington's breathing apparatus and thermal imagers. At the time, both Plaugher and D.C. Fire Chief Ronnie Few tried to minimize the issue, saying gear often gets mixed up on incident scenes.

In December 2001, however, Few claimed there was no evidence of the attempted theft and called for the investigation to be closed. That didn't fly with either the D.C. City Council or Plaugher, and according to the *Washington Post*, Few agreed later that month to reopen the probe…. If nothing else, the missing gear emphasizes the need for someone working logistics to track big-ticket gear at the scene.

Exercises—and futility

One may believe the answer to the question "Who's in charge?" is multiple-choice with only one right answer. In truth, it's an essay question that demands scholarship and forethought.

Forethought can prevent problems that at worst threaten lives and are at best awkward. Soon after the Pentagon attack, the order went out to close all the bridges connecting D.C., Virginia and Maryland. Then someone ordered tens of thousands of federal employees to go home, and "home" for most of them was across those same bridges.

Full-scale exercises offer one way to find such holes and fix them ahead of time. Not surprisingly, exercises such as the May 2000 TOPOFF(icials) revealed huge "who's-in-charge?" gaps. [The TOPOFF exercises were cosponsored by the Justice Department and the Federal Emergency Management Agency. The simulated events took place during 10 days in May 2000 and brought more than 100 senior staff members from 35 government agencies to the master control center. TOPOFF included three simulated terrorism scenarios: a chemical weapons incident in Portsmith, N.H.; a bioterrorism/medical crime in Denver; and a concurrent event involving nuclear devices in the Washington, D.C., area, called National Capital Region (NCR) 2000.] "I'll be blunt and say it this way: There's tension between the 'federalistas' and the state and local people," says Dr. John J. Hamre. Hamre, who was U.S. deputy secretary of defense 1997–99, is president and CEO of the Center for Strategic & International Studies. CSIS ran the Dark Winter bioterror exercise in June 2001. [For more information on this exercise, see http://www.homelandsecurity.org/darkwinter/index.cfm.]

"I was astounded at the gap in perceptions," he says. "Almost everybody at the federal level thought TOPOFF went pretty well. Everybody else thought the federalistas came in and were arrogant and took over and didn't listen. Neither side hears that about each other." (Hamre acknowledges his own 'federalista' status, by the way.)

Corey Gruber, for one, noted the tensions firsthand. Gruber is responsible for national exercises coordinated by the Office of Domestic Preparedness of the Department of Justice (DOJ). "One of the most important issues, it always is, is direction and control," Gruber said at a recent bioterror conference. "In TOPOFF, there were quite a few challenges in how we exchanged information among direction nodes, and a proliferation of those direction-control elements.

"If we have an incident command post established at an incident site, and you have a county emergency operations center, and then state and federal representatives at the incident command site, what happens to the county EOC? There were a considerable number of issues, and we took them to the point where people could see there were problems and things they would have to address."

Ah, but noting the problems and actually distributing them as lessons learned are two separate things. TOPOFF—good, bad and ugly—happened in May 2000.... The TOPOFF critique reportedly became mired in presidential-election politics and public-relations concerns as much as anything else. Gruber attributes the most recent delay to post-September security concerns.

Fortunately, others have published their own critiques of TOPOFF; one in the journal *Clinical Infectious Diseases* (Vol. 32, pages 436–445) covers the simulated bioattack on Denver. It's available at www.journals.uchicago.edu/cid/journal/issues. Authors Thomas V. Inglesby, Rita Grossman and Tara O'Toole opened their critique with—you guessed it—"who's in charge?" woes. "Issues surrounding leadership, the role of authorities, and the processes of decision-making were widely considered to be highly problematic and deserving of careful review," they wrote. "Overall, leadership roles and the role of authorities in the crisis were uncertain."

Examples the authors included (emphasis added):

- "Although the state public health agency was cited by some of the senior health participants as the agency with the highest authority in the exercise, ... other participants said *it was not clear who was in charge.*"

- "Another observer said *the FBI was operating under the assumption that the state attorney general's office was the organization with highest authority* because [it's the] ranking state office to which the FBI reports in a crisis."

- An ad hoc committee made (and often reversed) decisions both big and small based on hourly conference calls. "At some points, as many as 50–100 people participated in these calls; many participants had never previously met or worked together. The roles, authorities, and *even the identities* of those participating in the calls, as well as the leadership of and agendas for the calls, were unclear."

Conventional and chemical: From ICS to unified command

Let's return to the notion that "Who's in charge here?" presents as an essay question.

It's now common to hear about "WMD response tactics" and terms such as "b-nice" (biological, nuclear, incendiary, chemical, explosive); "CBNRE" (chemical, biological, nuclear, radiological, high energy; and "COBRA" (chemical, ordnance, biological, radiological/atomic), among plenty of others. The point not covered in those broad terms is this: The person in the hot seat for a chemical-weapon response almost certainly is not the right person to handle that job following a bioweapons attack.

"The issue of 'who's in charge?' means different things to different people in different situations," Briese says. "Take a conventional explosive, a truck bomb, a small bomb, not something that brings down an entire building, and the fire service would still likely be in charge of the emergency response in cooperation with local law enforcement."

For ongoing incidents, he says, the best incident commander might be the chief of the fire department. In some communities, someone other than the chief of the department (another fire officer or someone from law enforcement) might be the best choice.

Once an incident goes beyond a small device with a limited number of casualties, Briese says, the whole concept of "Who's in charge?" doesn't work. "Everyone's in charge of their own piece of the incident," he says. "That's why the concept of unified command is so important." Assuming an incident other than a bio attack, the first responder will establish incident command. As the incident grows, ICS develops into a unified command. That structure allows various agencies and personnel to plug into the existing operation, not start over from scratch, as they arrive.

Briese also emphasizes developing relationships before the question of command arises. "That need to plug in is why it's so important that the terrorism task forces in the FBI field offices, the one in Los Angeles is a great example, work together and learn how to cooperate at the local level," he says. "It's just not going to happen top-down; it's got to happen bottom-up."

Although Attorney General Ashcroft has increased the number of joint terrorism task forces, he can't dictate the human relations among individuals on the working groups. "It's taking the federal government a long time, but it's slowly understanding that the local level is the most important," Briese says. "The most we can do at the national level is facilitate local cooperation."

Briese acknowledges a point that has traditionally caused friction between the law-enforcement and fire communities. "From the very beginning, these types of incidents are crime scenes," he says. "The fire service is involved only to mitigate the emergency while preserving as much of the evidence as it can. Once the emergency is over and the casualties have been removed, it becomes strictly a crime scene and law enforcement takes the lead." That progression, incidentally, is how Plaugher describes the Pentagon response.

Bio: A whole different ballgame

Whether one prefers B-NICE, CBNRE, COBRA, or one of the other ever-evolving acronyms, it's the "B" part that demands the most attention these days. "We have to treat bio as a separate and distinct process from response to a high-explosive or chemical incident," says DOJ's Corey Gruber.

Bob Malson, president of the District of Columbia Hospital Association, offers first-hand observations about October's anthrax attacks and the response they garnered. "There is a distinction between most WMD events and biological events, and it's frequently lost at the outset and stays lost through most of the event. That distinction is that a bio event is constantly unfolding. In most other WMD events, when something goes boom, something falls, everybody is immediately a victim, a responder or an observer. In biological events, those roles all get mixed."

Every individual in a bio incident is a separate incident, Malson said, so all of the traditional incident-response mechanisms get left behind. "We're all better at managing that process than we were in October 2001," he says, "but we're not to the point yet where we'll all do the job we want to do."

Who's in charge of the media?

Without a clear message and appropriate messengers, a media frenzy can sometimes do more economic damage than the attacks themselves. Handling the media sits near the top of the command-and-control issues for WMD events.

"One of the things that was most commonly noted after TOPOFF, and we saw again for real after September 11," Gruber notes: "How do we organize ourselves to do joint public affairs? For the Pentagon incident, we didn't establish a joint information center, a JIC. It put a lot of pressure on the Arlington County incident commanders."

"In a bio incident," says Malson, operational importance "is an inverted pyramid, because the higher you go up in the constitutional process, the less control you have. The federal government doesn't have very many ambulances or hospitals, but the public expects the president or the secretary of HHS to be on the point."

Despite HHS Secretary Tommy Thompson's much-maligned anthrax comments early on, Hamre suggests that politicians must speak to the media (in concert with technical experts) during such crises. "There are issues that only our elected and appointed officials can speak credibly to the American public about," he contends. "Those are the safety issues, the larger sense of confidence in government."

The public's expectations, Malson says, present a challenge for the public information officer. "You need to...make sure you have police able to handle those questions and your medical people to handle those questions," he says.

"The even more complicated part is attempting to coordinate the political field, both vertically and horizontally. You have different counties, states and local jurisdictions, plus the federal arm, all trying to play out appropriately their various roles in an event that is constantly unfolding." Better make sure everyone's giving the media the same message; reporters use discrepancies in public statements to pit one agency against the other.

"We worry too much about who's in charge," Briese says. "Maybe in some cases, nobody's in charge and we just get the work done. If everybody understands what the roles and responsibilities are, we should be able to work together and get them done."

That may be good advice for, say, the balkanized fire departments in Prince George's County, Md., where firefighters occasionally come to blows about who's going to put out simple structure fires. For larger-scale incidents, a focus group assembled by the International Association of Fire Chiefs (IAFC) in 2002 offered a "preparedness objective."

Perhaps retired Chicago Fire Department hazmat legend John Eversole should have the final word (for the moment) about who should take the lead next time: "What it comes down to is this: Before an incident happens, you need to have a plan that details who does what and how they do it," Eversole says. "If you have a plan, you can adjust it to meet the specific needs of an incident. If you don't have a plan, you're just SOL."

10 | Emergency operations centers

Dave Douglas

An Amtrak train crashes into a freight train, derails and catches fire just outside Wendover, Utah, September 13, 2001. Many passengers are injured and in need of immediate medical care. Fortunately, none was killed.

In Texas, barges hit a piling and knock two 80-foot segments of the Queen Isabella Causeway into the Laguna Madre channel early Saturday, September 15, 2001. A third span crumbles and drops 85 feet into the water below, hours later. Anywhere between five and ten people are dead. Among the dead is Port Isabel Fire Chief Robert Harris, 46. The bridge was the only link between the mainland and South Padre Island, a popular resort on the Gulf of Mexico.

Most of us were riveted by television coverage of the September 11th horror in New York City. Yet, emergency management teams around the country were managing their own jurisdictions' responses to the tragedy in New York and the threat that it may visit their regions as well. There may also have been other major events in their own cities, counties and states.

Disasters can happen anywhere and, as so poignantly demonstrated in New York, it's our job to manage and mitigate them.

What drives an EOC?

In San Diego, the Emergency Operations Center (EOC) was activated within a few hours of the New York event. EOCs throughout the country became active to fulfill their obligation to the people they serve.

Like the term in real estate sales, "location, location, location," the catch phrase for emergency management is "preparation, preparation, preparation." Local and state emergency management officials work with the Federal Emergency Management Agency (FEMA) to prepare their jurisdictions for catastrophic events, a weapons of mass destruction attack, an airliner crash, major hazardous material spills, large fires, floods and storms. The list is limited only by our imagination and now, things we never imagined.

Staffing

EOCs are staffed by all departments within jurisdictions that are responsible for critical services. In many jurisdictions, these include Law Enforcement, Fire, Emergency Medical Services, Power and Gas, Streets or Highways department, Water services, Sewer, Governmental Management (City manager, County manager or Governor's Office) and Press Information. This constitutes a Unified Command structure. It is a unified team effort, which allows all agencies with responsibilities for the incident—either geographical or functional—to manage an incident by establishing a common set of

Originally published as "Emergency Management and Emergency Operations Centers," *Police*, Vol. 25, No. 11, pages 32–36, November, 2001. Published by Bobit Publishing Company, Torrance, California. Used with permission. Copyright Police Magazine (www.policemag.com).

objectives and strategies. This is accomplished without losing or abdicating their individual agencies' authority, autonomy, responsibility or accountability. EOCs are broken down into Command, Operations Planning, Logistics and Finance categories. The EOC participants are officials given the authority by their respective agencies to make decisions for that agency. In other words, the police official speaks with the authority of the chief; the fire official with the authority of the fire chief; the water utilities representative with the authority of the department head of that agency, etc.

Practice

Scenarios are dreamed up and plans are made to deal with those scenarios. Most agencies participate in drills in which the situations are broken down into time-lined events and then played out in real time to officials in the EOC. This is done to learn how they will handle the events as they come. Afterward, a team of experts critiques the whole situation. They look at what was done well and what areas require further work.

The most critical component of any EOC is communications. This is true not only for talking with their people in the field but with each person in the room as well. The people in the command center must be capable of communicating with one another. No shrinking violets are invited. They must be able to concisely tell their counterparts what their agencies' needs are and what they can do as the situation develops. The EOC commander must be able to turn to anyone in the room and immediately be informed of what that agency's current capabilities consist of.

Communication from the field is the lifeblood of any EOC operation. After all, if information on a given incident does not flow into the EOC, all you have is a bunch of officials sitting around in a dark room watching CNN on big screen television.

An EOC in action

Using mobile video technology from the field can be a force multiplier in the information battle for emergency management. During a recent event in San Diego, we used video from a number of different sources.

The FBI set up stationary cameras to monitor the area around our convention center. Video feeds from the sites were transmitted on fiber optic line directly into the EOC. We had live feeds from within the convention center using the center's in-place security cameras. This was accomplished using a video codec, an electronic device that compresses and packages video data for transmission on telephone lines supplied by the video conferencing vendor, RoseTel. We were able to use its existing RoseTel video conferencing system to view video in real time at the full 30 frames per second rate.

We used portable 2.4GHz spread-spectrum microwave transmitters attached to handheld cameras that sent a line of sight signal to a tall building in our downtown area and then retransmitted using fixed microwave equipment to the EOC. Additionally, we used GPS tracking microwave technology provided by Broadcast Microwave Services to transmit signals from both our police department helicopters' on-board camera/FLIR systems to our Headquarters building. The signal was then retransmitted to the EOC using the RoseTel Video Conferencing system.

Handheld receivers were passed out to the field commanders linking them to the helicopter video. This video gave the decision-makers the ability to see what was going on in the field and make decisions regarding personnel allocation based on real time information. Because of this, response time to incidents was cut drastically. Responding officers were able to get to a specific location quickly using routes that were reconnoitered using video and were able to bring the equipment appropriate for the situation. It was like having an invisible intelligence officer in the middle of the incident, communicating with the command staff. The EOC commander was able to have multiple views of the same incident and use the information to deliver assets that were appropriate for the situation.

Recovery phase

The final and equally important responsibility of the Emergency Management System is recovery. The job is not over when the threat or incident stops. Days, weeks or months may be involved. FEMA has many programs in place to assist local and state governments with clean-up and recovery. These include low interest rate government loan programs. The Public Assistance Program provides supplemental federal disaster grant assistance to help state and local governments and certain private non-profit organizations rebuild. There are individual assistance programs that assist people and businesses following a disaster and help them get back on their feet.

One of the ironies of EOC operations became highly visible September 11th. The address of The New York City Mayor's Office of Emergency Management was 7 World Trade Center—23rd Floor. It's another testament to Emergency Management personnel in New York that they were able to respond after the destruction of their center and rapidly open up a backup center to handle operations.

With the abrupt change experienced [after September 11], the emphasis on Emergency Management will surely grow. Gaining a working knowledge of the system is critical for all law enforcement personnel. If we know how the system works, we will be better able to respond to incidents and events as they occur. We will understand the capabilities of our jurisdiction's Emergency Management teams, what their needs are and how to communicate with them to satisfy our needs in the field.

Our hearts go out to all those in New York who were affected by the recent [World Trade Center] attack. They deserve the highest level of praise for their tremendous response to that unprecedented emergency.

11 Design of public buildings: Lessons learned

John Nicholson

For nearly an hour on September 11, the World Trade Center's twin towers still soared high above Manhattan, even after two hijacked jetliners had ripped into them, spewing thousands of gallons of burning jet fuel over several floors. The 244 closely spaced steel columns of the 100-story towers, the tallest buildings in New York City, held their own as smoke billowed from shattered walls and an inferno raged inside. On most floors, the steel columns still formed the towers' exteriors.

At 9:50 a.m., however, the 1,362-foot (415-meter) south tower collapsed in a tragic display of terror. About a half-hour later, the 1,368-foot (417-meter) north tower went down.

What had finally reduced the well-constructed towers, which had survived a terrorist bombing in a basement parking garage in 1993, to a pile of concrete and steel about 12 stories high?

A number of engineers, including building experts of the National Fire Protection Association (NFPA), believe each tower could have withstood the impact of a single large airplane, as they were designed to. Once the 24,000 gallons (91,000 liters) of aviation fuel in each Boeing 767 exploded into flames, however, it was just a matter of time before the towers collapsed, they say.

"A determination will have to be made as to the combinations of the loss of structural support from the initial impact of the aircraft, coupled with the heat from the resulting fires that ultimately resulted in the collapse," says Robert E. Solomon, NFPA's chief building fire protection engineer. "The heat from the jet fuel fires, which are estimated to have reached temperatures of 2,000°F (1,093°C) are well above temperatures that can reduce the structural strength of steel trusses used to hold up the concrete slab floors."

"As an engineer," says Bonnie Manley, NFPA's structural engineer, "I was thankful to see the buildings still standing, but I knew it wasn't beyond the realm of possibility that they'd collapse. One floor collapsed and then the other in what's called a 'pancake failure'—one floor falling down on the other."

To maximize the space inside the buildings, the towers were designed with a column-free interior supported by an inner core of steel columns and the tubular steel that ringed the structures. The aircrafts' impact, the explosion, and the heat from the resulting fires may have weakened the steel girders until they could no longer support the weight above them. As one floor collapsed into another, the structures collapsed inwardly, minimizing damage to the surrounding area. The tower collapsed downward. The design helped prevent extensive damage to neighboring buildings, says Manley.

Originally published as "Collapse: World Trade Center Aftermath." Reprinted with permission from NFPA Journal (Vol. 95, No. 6) copyright 2001, National Fire Protection Association, Quincy, MA. All rights reserved.

Sprinkler system overwhelmed

In a conventional fire, the towers' sprinkler systems would have been sufficient to control the blaze, but these unconventional fires overwhelmed the suppression systems.

"In a normal office setting, there's quite a bit of material that can feed a fire, but adding the aviation fuel created a fire that was far larger and hotter than a normal system could handle," Manley notes.

As a result, there was never enough water to stop the fires.

According to David Hague, NFPA's senior fire protection engineer, the initial impacts probably rendered the sprinkler and stand-pipe systems inoperative on the fire floors and displaced any fire-resistance coatings on the structural steel. This exposed the steel to temperatures in the range of 1,600°F (871°C) and higher.

Even if the fire protection systems had remained operative, it's unlikely they'd have discharged enough water to protect the structural steel, he says.

"We can design systems to cope with the fire loading presented by such quantities of jet fuel—it's done constantly in aircraft hangars," Hague notes. "But the system would be a foam-water system, and a foam-water system isn't practical for buildings of this type. Water has some effect on jet fuel, but it's not as effective as a foam-water system."

Hague adds that he can't advocate a foam-water sprinkler system for this type of occupancy simply to prepare for the possibility of impact from an aircraft.

"The money would be better spent on security," he says.

Safety by design

Dedicated in 1973 after five years of construction, the towers had 10 million square feet (929,003 square meters) of office space. They were owned by the Port Authority of New York and New Jersey, and were designed by Michigan-based Minoru Yamasaki Associates Inc., and Emery Roth and Sons of New York.

When engineers design a building, they calculate the loads and forces to which the building will be subjected over its lifetime. Typically, these include the effects of hurricanes, impact, winds, floods, earthquakes, and, in taller buildings, plane strikes.

The World Trade Center was designed to withstand a lot of stress, even a direct hit from a Boeing 707, which was the state-of-the-art jetliner at the time it was designed. The impact of a large plane and resulting jet fuel fire were factored into the towers' design as a result of lessons learned in 1945 when an Army Air Force B-25 crashed into the Empire State Building in heavy fog. Fourteen people died, and damage to the building, which was hit between the 79th and 80th floors, came to $1 million. The building's structural integrity wasn't affected.

According to Manley, the towers' designers took into account all types of extremes when they drew up the plans for the World Trade Center more than 30 years ago. However, "there was no way to imagine that this collapse would ever happen when the buildings were designed," she says.

The towers' design has been described by the American Society of Civil Engineers as a "series of load-bearing exterior columns spaced 3 feet (91 centimeters) apart and tied together at every floor by a deep horizontal beam, creating a strong lattice of square tubing around each tower." Special plates were placed among the buildings' trusses to reduce stress caused by winds up to 200 miles (322 kilometers) per hour.

The twin towers also had the world's highest load-bearing walls, designed by Seattle-based structural engineer Worthington, Skilling, Helle, and Roberston as vertical, cantilevered steel tubes. Exterior columns were hollow box sections 14 inches (35-centimeters) square spaced 39 inches (99 centimeters) on center. Spandrels welded to the columns at each floor created huge trusses. This gave the towers, each of which measured 208 by 208 feet (63 by 63 meters), a column-free interior between the outer walls and the 79-by-139-foot (24-by-42-meter) core.

The core surrounding each building's 99 elevators also consisted of a lattice of steel covered by concrete that connected the interior columns to the exterior. Staircases in the buildings were designed to be evacuated in an hour, according to published reports. Each tower also had five underground parking levels.

Redundancy was also a part of the design. Redundancy in a building provides multiple load patterns for dissipating gravity and environmental loads.

"If one link breaks in that chain, the chain no longer functions; however, redundancy means that there are several more chains available to pick up a share of the load that was once carried by the chain," says Manley.

Such safeguards slowed the buildings' eventual collapse and provided occupants more time to evacuate, saving many lives. Eventually, however, the redundant systems were, like the fire suppression system, overwhelmed.

"What happened was completely unexpected, and this extreme situation overwhelmed the systems," says Manley.

What now?

Will future design standards and building codes take into account events such as the attack of the World Trade Center? NFPA experts working on NFPA 5000, *Building Code*™, don't believe the new code will reference the incident, but there will be a greater sense of awareness within the building community that things such as this can happen.

Following the 1995 bombing of the Alfred P. Murrah Federal Building in Oklahoma City, there was a great deal of discussion about what it would take to destroy a building, but that stopped when experts realized that terrorists could quickly override any standards proposed. When it comes to terrorist attacks, what a building can withstand won't be defined, Manley says.

"Standards, such as those in blast engineering, aren't specific. You can't define the loading because once you do, someone will come up with a way to overcome it," says Manley.

Can engineers design terrorist-resistant buildings? Maybe, but they would probably resemble fortresses, and people might not use them or be able to afford them.

Which leaves the option of increased security. Among the methods engineers use to enhance building security are reinforced structural frames and perimeters, Kevlar curtains or bullet-proof glass, fewer windows, and more secure entrances. Designs can also eliminate or restrict vehicle access and parking. All of these options will doubtless come into play in the future design and construction of public buildings, particularly high rises. It's too early to know how the lessons learned at such a cost in the attack on the World Trade Center will change the way things are done on many levels, some we can't yet envision.

12 | Security for public utilities

Beth Wade

When Milwaukee Water Works began planning for security upgrades in 1999, terrorism was not part of the picture. "We were thinking about vandals and graffiti artists and unhappy current and former employees," says Carrie Lewis, superintendent for the agency. "We thought that the most serious attacker could be a local with a political agenda, somebody like Timothy McVeigh. The international, organized, funded terrorist was not something we thought about."

The Water Works' main treatment plant is situated close to Lake Michigan and abuts soccer fields, beaches and a marina. The city lately has improved public access to the lakefront, increasing visitation to the area—and visibility of the water plant. "Every now and then, a bicyclist would end up on plant grounds, or a soccer player would walk in to see what the place was," Lewis explains. "The fact that those people were getting onto the plant grounds made us realize that we had to tighten up."

By the time Sept. 11, 2001, arrived, Milwaukee Water Works was ahead of the security curve. It had completed a system-wide evaluation and had begun implementing measures to mitigate its risks.

Most public water systems (there are 168,000 in the United States) were not as well positioned as Milwaukee's. As a result, those communities are gearing up for their own security evaluations, which will include identifying assets, assessing vulnerability and risk, considering countermeasures and weighing costs.

Three major concerns

Assessing vulnerability begins with identifying assets (e.g., people, equipment, facilities) and potential threats to those assets. Evaluation must be comprehensive, says Brian Ramaley, director of Newport News (Va.) Waterworks. "[Utilities] have to look at their entire systems, from stem to stern, from the headwaters to the customer's tap, and determine where their systems are most vulnerable," he notes.

Furthermore, the evaluation should focus on activity rather than on the attacker. As Lewis noted, attackers can come in many forms—from employees and vandals to renegades and terrorists—but threats to the water system are limited to what those people can do.

Activities can range from low-level intrusion, such as that described by Lewis, to more serious acts that interrupt operations or even sicken or kill residents. The major threats fall within the realm of physical damage to facilities, cyber attack and system contamination.

Originally published as "Locking Down on Water System Security," this article first appeared in the January 2002 edition of American City & County magazine (www.americancityandcounty.com) and is republished here with permission of the publisher. Copyright 2002, Primedia Business Magazines & Media, Inc. All rights reserved.

Physical damage

Damage or destruction of equipment and facilities, including pumps, pipelines and tanks, can affect any component of a water system, from source and transmission to storage and distribution. How is the intake protected? Where are pipelines exposed? How are tank hatches secured? What is the backup for a facility that is completely destroyed? Those are the types of questions that have to be answered during vulnerability assessments, says Mark Knudson, director of operations and maintenance for the Portland Water Bureau.

Cyber attack

With the advent of supervisory control and data acquisition (SCADA) systems, water utilities have moved steadily from manual to automated operation. What happens if a hacker disables the SCADA system?

"Most water systems in America are able to run in a fully manual mode, although perhaps not as efficiently as we operate with our computer monitoring and control systems," Ramaley says. "Were those systems compromised through some form of cyber attack, there's little doubt that we could continue to function and meet the needs of our customers."

"For most of us, if the system shuts down, we can run it manually," confirms John Sullivan, chief engineer for the Boston Water and Sewer Commission and president of the Association of Metropolitan Water Agencies, based in Washington, D.C. "The real question is: Does anybody know how to do it? When you build a new plant and everything runs by computer, do the operators ever simulate [manual operations]?"

Sullivan also notes that communities with automated security sometimes integrate those systems with the SCADA network. Having both systems on one server presents a two-for-one hit for a hacker.

Contamination

Much of the attention given to water system contamination has focused on system-wide contamination using biological, chemical and radiological agents. However, in October 2001, U.S. Environmental Protection Administration Administrator Christie Whitman stated that contamination with system-wide implications is unfeasible.

"People are worried that a small amount of some chemical or biological agent—a few drops, for instance—could result in significant threats to the health of large numbers of people," she said. "That scenario just can't happen. It would take large amounts of contaminants to threaten the safety of a city water system."

Vulnerability to contamination still has to be assessed, according to Knudson. "If we look at source water, there might be a concern about contamination that's going to find its way to intake," he notes. "If [the source] is a well field, there are geohydrology issues: What happens if [we discover a contaminant] in one well? Will it show up in another one? In the transmission system, contamination is an issue because there are probably places where you could contaminate an open channel or aqueduct."

Assessing vulnerability

Vulnerability studies can be performed by utility staff or by a third party, but, ideally, they are done by both. "Outside studies are more likely to pick up things that you would miss in house," Ramaley says. "But you can't just sit back and wait to bring in the experts. You have to look at things yourself and then bring in the outside, fresh eyes to look at your system."

"It really has to be both," Knudson says. "Nobody knows the system as well as the people who have to make it work. Those are the people that are the operators and the engineers that deal with the system on a day-to-day basis. At the same time, because they deal with it every day, they are [not necessarily objective]. You need the objective opinion of the consultant."

When Milwaukee Water Works conducted its vulnerability assessment, it worked with Sandia National Laboratories, based in Albuquerque, N.M. The laboratory had been hired by the Denver-based American Water Works Association Research Foundation to study water system vulnerabilities and produce a guide for utilities to conduct their own assessments. It selected Milwaukee as its "guinea pig," Lewis says.

"We were in the right place at the right time," she says. "For two years, we had budgeted money to upgrade security at our facilities. Sandia gave us some specific advice on what they had seen while they were here.[2]

"Some of the recommendations were easy fixes, like making sure that hatch locks are not the kind that bolt cutters can cut," Lewis notes. "Others, like upgrading electronic surveillance and alarm systems, [were more involved]."

Sullivan favors bringing in a third party, too. "I'm not saying it has to be a consultant's paradise, but you need to bring in an outside consultant to get a fresh pair of eyes. You need a Doubting Thomas," he says. "You need the other person there to ask, 'Why do you leave all your tools for your pump right in front of the pump?' Well, you do that because [the pump has] odd-sized bolts, and the tools are only good for that pump. You're thinking the tools are there to fix the pump, and the consultant is thinking, 'No. Those tools are there to destroy the pump.'"

Nationwide, consulting firms are gearing up to assist with vulnerability assessments. "You've got security experts who know nothing about water and water experts who know nothing or very little about security," Ramaley cautions. "It's really critical that anybody who does this type of work has both sets of expertise and knows how to marry that up so you get useful results."

Determining risk

Every water system has vulnerabilities, but vulnerability does not equal risk. To determine risk, utilities have to review their vulnerability findings and measure the probability of an attack.

"You have to decide what's important to you and then determine the chances of people getting at it," Sullivan says. He notes that an earthen dam may pose vulnerability, but, if it is not easily accessible, it is not necessarily a risk.

Furthermore, utilities should look at risk in light of potential consequences. "You need to take a look at your system and ask, 'What would happen if this went out?'" Sullivan explains. "For example, 'If I lose this pump, what happens?' Maybe the answer is, 'Nothing. I've got another one over on the other side of town, and I'll pump on that one.' But that is where you have to measure your risk."

Having determined their risks, utilities must be prepared to live with some of them, Knudson says. "We're not going to be able to completely eliminate all the risks associated with potential vulnerabilities," he notes. "We just can't afford to do it. We could spend billions of dollars on any given system, and we would still not be there. You have to ask—and here's the key to the whole thing—'What level of risk are we willing to accept?'"

More than anything, that exercise can help utilities focus their countermeasures. "It gives you the information you need to make an informed decision about where you want to spend your money," Knudson explains. "You might decide that it doesn't make sense to put armed guards out at the wellhead because you don't think the wellhead [poses a great risk]. But that becomes a conscious decision in terms of accepting risk."

Mitigating risk

Armed guards? Actually, many of the recommendations for mitigating risk are far more mundane.

"Everyone's facilities were built with doors and gates and windows that lock," Lewis says. "The first thing is to use those things that are already available to us, and the second thing is to get the buy-in of your employees. Those are the people who are at the facilities around the clock, and they can assess whether something they see or hear is unusual and alert others [for response]."

Employees also have to buy in to security procedures, Knudson says. "They have to understand the necessity of keeping doors locked and understand that, if somebody walks up, you don't just let them in."

Public access is a thing of the past, according to Ramaley. Utilities that offered facility tours have, since Sept. 11, locked down. "Many systems have eliminated that," Ramaley notes. "They've shut their gates; they've locked their doors."

Detection and delay

In addition to making those changes, water utilities are upgrading security by installing surveillance equipment, and expanding fencing and setbacks, with emphasis on detecting the adversary and delaying him. "I think it's unreasonable to expect every single water utility to upgrade its defenses to successfully defend against organized, armed terrorists," Lewis says. "I think we need to tighten up our facilities so that the casual and lower-level attackers will either go someplace else, or we can delay them long enough to detect them."

Detection is part of the plan in Newport News. There, the Waterworks is considering expansion of electronic surveillance, and it has stepped up watershed patrols. "We serve five jurisdictions, and our facilities touch seven jurisdictions. We've coordinated with local law enforcement in each of those jurisdictions to visit our facilities on a regular basis," Ramaley says. "We've also [contacted] the local FBI office, and I recommend that all water utilities consider doing that. If there is a problem, you're going to have to work with those folks, and it's good to know them ahead of time and have those communication channels open."

Delivery and recovery

Newport News also has worked with chemical suppliers to boost security on deliveries. "Alum deliveries come to us in large tanks. Those trucks are now sealed before they leave the chemical shipping lot, and the seal is not broken until it gets to our site," he says. Similarly, prior to receiving chemicals, Milwaukee Water Works gets the serial number of the tanker and the driver's name from the supplier, and it checks both before accepting delivery.

Although many mitigation measures focus on prevention, others focus on recovery. "Mitigation is sometimes a matter of keeping a spare piece of equipment," Lewis says. "Historically, our inventory was [managed on an as-needed basis]; if you've got eight pumps in a room and one goes out, the other seven will run, so you can wait two months to get parts for the broken one. But now we're operating under the scenario of someone taking out all the pumps, so we will keep the parts that we can in inventory."

Design implications

In addition to upgrading security in the short term, water utilities are anticipating changes in technology and facility design that could help them mitigate risk. The water industry is pushing for research and development of microtoxicity monitors and gas chromatographs that could help utilities pinpoint contaminants in their systems. Additionally, new plants will be built with security in mind.

"I think every facility built from now on will be looked at totally different," Sullivan says. "You'll see brick walls, sky lights with bars. You won't just have door alarms; you'll have backup systems—maybe a door and a camera or an infrared [detection device]."

"Security will be incorporated much more completely in terms of alarms and lighting and typical security-type measures," confirms Les Lampe, vice president and director of water resources for Black & Veatch, a Kansas City, Mo.–based consultant. "You're going to see a lot more focus on setback spaces; you're going to see fewer entrances; and you're going to see more control over the roadways, gates, fences and lighting."

Utilities will be looking for optimum safety of source supplies, making them less open and available for contamination, Lampe says. He also expects to see more attention to alternative treatment processes that might provide a higher level of protection than do conventional processes.

"There are a lot of design implications as a result of security concerns," Ramaley says. "We have to look at our facilities as needing to be able to withstand or continue to provide service under potential attack, or at least to know where, if we were attacked, we would be most likely to fail and how we would recover from that quickly. It's not going to be possible to harden all of our facilities so that they can't be attacked, but we can lay our systems out so that recovery can be much quicker."

Quick recovery requires redundancy, and Lampe reports that he is seeing increased emphasis on redundancy, from SCADA backup to power feeds for pump stations. He also notes that physical separation of facilities can assist with recovery. "If you have one pumping facility that is critical to your whole system, [it may be possible] to add smaller pumping stations in different locations, giving you reliability without putting everything in one location," he explains.

Finding funding

From vulnerability and risk assessments to mitigation, shoring up the nation's water systems will be expensive. Where will the money come from?

Congress has debated two bills that could help substantially with payment for assessments and future technology. The first, passed by the House in November, 2001, appropriates more than $109 million to assist communities with vulnerability assessments. The second bill proposed $60 million for research and development of monitoring technology.

Those sums will not cover security costs for every water system, however. As a result, Sullivan anticipates that cities will share information, with bigger cities assisting smaller ones. "The small guys, who might not have the money for consultants, could work off the big guys," he suggests.

Water utilities may have to raise rates to recoup some of their costs, and they will definitely have to weigh the feasibility of security spending against the capital requirements for infrastructure repairs, adding capacity and complying with regulations.

There is a long road ahead, Ramaley says. "Securing our water systems is going to be a long process," he notes. "It's one that we need to begin immediately, and there is going to be an economic price to be paid. Utilities are going to have to begin down the path and keep moving towards more and more secure facilities."[3]

Editor's notes:

[1] *Water System Security: A Field Guide* was published by the American Water Works Association in 2002. It describes measures a water utility can take for better security against manmade threats. See http://www.awwa.org/bookstore.

[2] A videotape is available from the American Water Works Association entitled "Security Risk Assessment for Water Utilities." It is a videotape of a November 2001 teleconference reporting on research conducted by Sandia National Laboratories for the AWWA Research Foundation. It is designed to help utilities assess their security systems and develop measures to reduce risks and mitigate the consequences of terrorist or other criminal attacks. See http://www.awwa.org//bookstore.

[3] In 2003 the White House released a *National Strategy for the Physical Protection of Critical Infrastructures and Key Assets.* See http://www.whitehouse.gov/pcipb/physical.html.

13 | Evacuation planning for high-rise buildings

David R. Blossom

Life affords no higher pleasure than that of surmounting difficulties, passing from one step of success to another, forming new wishes, and seeing them gratified. He that labors in any great or laudable undertaking has his fatigues first supported by hope and afterwards rewarded by joy.
—Samuel Johnson

It is indeed difficult at this time to think of words such as "success," "gratification," or "joy" in the aftermath of the tragedy of September 11, 2001. If we look at our history, we would see that woven in our very fabric is the thread of overcoming adversity and becoming stronger and better for it. We have been handed just such an opportunity. Those people whose lives were taken from this earth will cry out that we learn and become better through their sacrifice. This we must do and do well.

In the aftermath of the attack on our country, the only way to put the pieces together is to look for the opportunity created by such destruction.

Two glaring facts have stood out as a result of this incident: (1) We have expected too much of our firefighters in asking them to fight fires in buildings that are too tall, and (2) we have woefully underestimated the high-rise evacuation issue.

Nothing in this selection is intended to presume facts about the events at the World Trade Center (WTC) on September 11. The observations included here are based on known facts and initial reports of those who experienced this tragedy. It is also beyond the scope of this article to explore in detail issues related to training and preparation requirements for high-rise safety. One thing that must be kept in mind is that the collapse of the two towers [or any high-rise], as occurred on September 11, was beyond what our collective minds could comprehend as a possibility, although Chief Donald Anthony of the Los Angeles City (CA) Fire Department had predicted such a possibility after the First Interstate Bank fire more than 10 years ago. We will never again look at a raging fire in such a building in the same way.

What is a high-rise?

Over the past 100 years, we have wrestled with the high-rise issue. We finally settled on the definition of a high-rise contained in National Fire Protection Association Standard 101, *Life Safety Code*® "a building greater than 75 feet in height." This definition beat out "100 feet" and "highest aerial apparatus available." I have a friend who has his own definition: "any building that is too high to jump from and survive." I have no quarrel with the definition that has been applied. However, I have identified a serious flaw of not carrying the *Life Safety Code*® definition to the next step.

Just how far above 75 feet? The number of feet higher has made little difference in our thinking. Yet, I believe we will all agree there is a big difference between 100 feet

Originally published as "High-Rise Safety: Have We Missed the Obvious?" Reprinted from *Fire Engineering*, Vol. 155, No. 1, pages 75–83, January, 2002. Published by Fire Engineering, Fair Lawn, New Jersey. Reprinted with permission of *Fire Engineering*.

higher and 1,300 feet higher. How did we not recognize this glaring gap in our approach to high-rise safety? I believe it is because, until September 11, a high-rise collapse was not possible—at least, in our thinking. The result of our not addressing this issue to the fullest is that we have built buildings that cannot be evacuated easily and quickly. We have also demanded that our firefighters fix the problem when it occurs, even if it is 1,000 feet in the air and the only way up is by stairs.

Excessive evacuation time

Many studies have been done and formulas have been developed to help us determine a reasonable projection of the time for evacuating a high-rise structure. (I will not explain or defend here any particular method of calculation.) It has been estimated that it would take in excess of two hours and under four hours—not considering special needs—to evacuate occupants from a 110-story structure. One evacuee of One World Trade Center indicated that it had taken him 50 minutes to egress from the 71st floor. Yet, in the 1993 bombing incident at the WTC, we know that it took up to six hours to evacuate the entire building. We also do not calculate the reduction of egress capacity for the portion of the stairways and exits firefighters are using to enter the building, thus reducing exit capacity.

There is no indication of the time lapse between the start of the incident and the decision to evacuate. It is also difficult to take into consideration the nature of a particular incident. Indeed, it would be difficult for building and life safety codes to address such a massive assault of two structures such as occurred in the WTC on September 11. It is highly likely that the protected means of egress for floors above the impact points were compromised and unavailable to those occupants on the highest floors. There is no possible way to predict or prepare for the alternative evacuation routes needed in such situations.

Our high-rise history has dictated that the building will protect us while we evacuate and mount firefighting activity. It is more important that we address the practicality of evacuation for points below the impact areas, which we assume were intact and available for egress. The sheer height of such a building would, without consideration of the emergency situation, affect the occupants' ability to egress in time to be removed to a safe area outside the building. This raises the question: Can we justify such tall structures from which there is no reasonable expectation that we can evacuate occupants within the time available to maintain structural integrity?

In the case of the WTC towers, some articles reported the fire rating to be two hours. Under "normal" conditions, this may even be increased to three hours or longer. Certainly, this level of protection did not take into consideration such a massive fire load introduced from outside the building, nor should it have. Without any doubt, it is almost impossible to believe that towers of such strength could have succumbed so quickly. I tend to agree with one commentator who stated that we should not be so amazed that the buildings failed so soon but that they stood for so long.

The question of how high we should build will haunt us after this tragedy and no doubt will be factored into the planning of new high-rise buildings.

Occupant response and evacuation

In my opinion, there are three essential components to evacuation issues: occupant preparedness, permission to evacuate, and capability. In some parts of the country, people have become quite accustomed to working and living in high-rise buildings. However, the conveniences of elevators have caused them to ignore the stairways. Keeping the fact that the stairways exist in the back of their minds does not make them familiar with the process of using the stairs to evacuate the building.

Stair enclosures often are not air-conditioned, are poorly illuminated, are filled with dust and dirt, are all too often used for storage, and are poorly maintained. The stairway is not an area occupants would normally think about. Nor would they think about using the stairway to practice evacuation from time to time.

Most of us subscribe to the theory that catastrophic events happen to someone else, not us, which adds to the indifference concerning the "system" of egressing from a high-rise. Over the life span of a building, the stairs may be needed only a few times for evacuation purposes.

An often overlooked factor pertaining to evacuation is that while the occupants are using the stairs to evacuate, a stream of diligent warriors will be rushing into the building using the same protected passage occupants are using to escape, making it more difficult to exit. This is an aspect of high-rise design with which we must cope.

Permission to evacuate

Permission to evacuate is of great concern. Almost from the beginning of the WTC incident, building occupants related their initial response was based on an initial feeling that they were in some danger—that "something" had just happened. They didn't rely on notification from alarms or some other mechanical means. One occupant stated that he felt the impact and then decided to go to another floor, where his wife worked. They met and decided to return to their offices. He later reported that he had made it out but did not know where his wife was.

Another occupant said he was aware that something was wrong and went around checking windows before finally going to his superior to ask if they should evacuate because something may be wrong. It was further reported that, after the first attack, one supervisor asked his employees in the unaffected tower to return to their workstations, obviously unaware of the danger that would befall them in less than 20 minutes.

One Fire Department of New York chief reported finding 50 employees huddled near the 70th floor just before the second collapse and ordered them to get out just a few minutes before the second collapse. Clearly, we have not done enough to educate high-rise occupants so that they can make the right decision, or we have taught them too well to rely on the building fire alarm sound and/or automatic directions from the fire alarm voice communication system.

In [the WTC] situation, the occupants did not appear to be able to or want to make a decision to evacuate the building. People often look for leadership in emergencies.

Have we considered the importance of panic? Yes, panic! It would be difficult for anyone to believe that such tall and strong structures could ever collapse; it seems reasonable to believe that we would be safe as long as we are away from the fire area. The standard operating procedure has been to evacuate the fire floor, the floors above, and two floors below. The question remains, Why have we not given permission to high-rise occupants (or occupants of any other buildings for that matter) to seek safety in the face of possible danger?

Neil Townsend, divisional officer, London Fire Brigade, puts it this way: "I think that when people die in fires, it's not because of panic—it's more likely to be the lack of panic."

I know that this statement flies in the face of what we have told ourselves.

Professor David Canter, of Liverpool University, may have put it in a more acceptable way: "You must think about people's reactions to a fire in terms of the three basic stages of making sense of what's going on, preparing to act, and then acting." There seems to be some breakdown in these areas.

The capability to effectively exit a high-rise depends on many factors; physical capability is only one of the important considerations. Capability hinges greatly on the two issues: Have the occupants made an attempt to become familiar with the protected means of egress from the building? If so, do they understand what to do if they feel a need to use that means of egress? Are they capable of making the right decisions and acting on those decisions when faced with such threats?

Capability also relies on the ability to understand what is going on around you. Initially, many of the occupants in this situation had very little information to process to make the decisions they needed to make. This situation changed as they received calls from the outside with new information.

Types of evacuation

The most common theories on egress have held that high-rise situations call for two basic types of evacuation: self-evacuation of the total building and controlled selective evacuation.

Self-evacuation, which takes on a life of its own, is essentially a haphazard process. It is based entirely on the decisions and actions carried out by large segments of building occupants. Controlled selective evacuation requires that the building's management have input in the decision-making process and execution of the actions needed to evacuate and that those responsible for evacuating occupants are adequately trained to make the right decisions and provide the leadership to achieve a successful outcome. A controlled selective evacuation should also be coordinated with the local fire department.

Elements in perceiving an emergency

Essentially six elements are involved in the perception of a fire incident or other emergency: recognition, validation, definition, evaluation, commitment, and reassessment.

- Recognition occurs when the individual perceives that there is a threat. This perception is achieved through multiple inputs, including visual and audible alarms, the smell of smoke, and a loud noise.

- The above signs lead to validation of the input and raise questions such as the following: What is the source of the sign I recognized? Is the input validated according to my perception?

- The process of definition is more complicated. This is the point at which the individual begins to relate to the validated recognition and moves into action. This is also the point at which anxiety can surface, dependent on the ability to process the information. There is a very narrow timeframe between this stage and the point at which the individual makes an evaluation.

- During the evaluation phase, cognitive and psychological activities motivate the individual to respond to the threat. This is the point at which the initial decision pertaining to course of action is made. If the right decisions have been made, taking planned action can quell anxiety.

- During the commitment stage, the individual decides the course of action based on the initial input. Individuals will complete, partially complete, or abandon their strategy. If they could not make the right decisions, they will return to the initial stages of their reaction and begin the process all over again until they are successful or fail completely.

- Anxiety and defeat can become overpowering in the reassessment stage. If the initial attempts fail, the individuals will become more frustrated, and anxiety will build. To achieve the desired results, the individual must process the relevant information correctly and take the right action. Individuals meeting with success will continue with their plans.

Some considerations here include the following: Have we done all that we can to educate the general public and occupants of high-rise buildings? Do occupants know what to expect in an emergency? Have we given them permission to act in their best interest and the interests of their fellow occupants by moving to a safe area? Have we provided the training that will help them to make the right choices and act accordingly? Have we failed to recognize that the height of the buildings we construct should be that which the great engineering minds can design to stand?

These questions will become more important as we consider the tragic events in New York City and evaluate the potential for occupants in similar situations to respond properly. While we pray that we never again will have to face another such horrific incident that will afford us only one chance to respond correctly, it would be a dishonor to those who perished if we do not take the lessons learned and develop answers that will help others in the future.

Evacuation training and firefighting operations

The *Life Safety Code®* and regulations of the Department of Labor's Occupational Safety and Health Administration (OSHA) dictate minimum requirements for occupant training and drills for the workplace. The major difference between the two is that the *Life Safety Code®* is concerned with building occupants, whereas OSHA requirements are directed toward the desired actions employers should take to protect their employees' safety. The main concerns outlined in the OSHA requirements are directed toward the nature of the hazard, recognition of hazards, controls or protective measures, engineering controls, administrative controls, and personal protection controls.

Both the *Life Safety Code®* and OSHA requirements are driven by the concept of the owner/management as the source of responsibility for compliance. Enforcement of these requirements often is sporadic and varies greatly from region to region. High-rise management typically is not aware of what it is required to do and often will resist when "forced" to do something through enforcement procedures alone. Management is much more receptive when it is educated about the requirements and how to comply. Because of this lack of understanding, it is not uncommon for high-rise occupants to be left on their own to respond when an emergency occurs.

Another area in which we have seen little change is firefighting operations. We have demanded that fire department personnel carry tremendous loads of equipment up an excessive number of flights of stairs and then expect them to be capable of initiating firefighting activity—higher and higher into the sky without appreciating the physical demands of just arriving at the fire floor, let alone being able to initiate the strenuous physical activity of rescue, fire attack, extinguishment, and overhaul.

Previous attempts to develop methods of exterior access on upper floors of high-rise buildings have not been practical or successful. Platforms suspended from helicopters have had limited ability to carry personnel and equipment. Landing firefighters on building roofs has also been largely impractical, as this places lives above the fire floor in the direction in which the fire is traveling. There has been some limited success with this approach; however, for large-scale operations, this usually is not an option.

Where does that leave us? Do we stick with what we have, or do we look for other solutions?

Occupant training requirements

One of the challenges we encounter when attempting to decide the training and drill requirements applicable to high-rise occupancies involves making a determination as to the type of occupancy with which we are dealing. On the surface, a high-rise such as the WTC would appear to be nothing more than a high-rise business occupancy, defined in the *Life Safety Code®* as "an occupancy used for account and record keeping or the transaction of business other than mercantile." One of the examples given is "General Offices." This seems to fit our needs fairly well. However, on reviewing the requirements in the "Operating Features Section for Business Occupancies," we discover that the only distinction for these requirements is that there be an employee population of either 500 total or more than 100 persons above or below the street level. There, again, is no distinction between one level or 100 levels above street level and anything in between.

We then must determine our occupant load for the building in question. If we use the square footage in Table 7.3.1.2 of the *Life Safety Code®*, we would divide our building area by 100. Thus for one level of the WTC, we would determine the occupancy to be 300 per floor, with some consideration for areas such as elevators, storage, service, and so on. This would result in a total occupant load of approximately 33,000 per tower building. This may be too few based on some reports of the actual building population. In this situation, we may be expecting far fewer occupants than there really are.

A review of the "Operating Features" section for New and Existing Business Occupancies reveals that occupants must be trained in accordance with Section 4.7 Fire Drills. The training requirements include knowledge of the following:

- the purpose of emergency egress and relocation drills
- the building's fire safety features
- the egress facilities available, and
- evacuation procedures.

In addition, occupants must be given the opportunity for instruction, and practice drills should be provided.

There is also a requirement for employee training in the use of the fire extinguisher, although this is not supported in many areas where the fire department preference is for evacuation only.

Clearly, specific training objectives must be achieved. It should be noted that there are no additional requirements based on the business being located in a high-rise.

Requirements under the Department of Labor are found in OSHA 29 CFR 1910.38, *Employee Emergency Plans and Fire Prevention Plans*. OSHA offers guidelines to assist employers with identifying training needs. Section 1910.1200 outlines some basics of worker fire- and life-safety practices. OSHA offers in section 1910.157 the following choices concerning employees and portable fire extinguisher training:

- Option 1: Total evacuation of all employees once an alarm has sounded. The employer in selecting this option must establish an emergency action plan and fire prevention plan.

- Option 2: Designated employees who have been trained to use portable fire extinguishers may use them to fight fires. Employees not selected and trained to do so must evacuate the area immediately once an alarm has sounded. The employer must create the prevention and emergency plan and comply with requirements for the inspection, testing, and maintenance of the fire extinguishers in addition to providing the training and education.

- Option 3: Applies the above requirements to all employees of the business.

It should be noted that the training must include the elements of hands-on practice under simulated emergency conditions. As a minimum, the fire extinguisher training must include the discharging of fire extinguishers.

In many areas of the country, the fire service disapproves of Options 2 and 3. The preference is for employees to evacuate the building, leaving any and all firefighting activity to trained firefighters. On the surface, this approach appears to be the most rational solution. It contains the element of having the building partially or completely evacuated by the time the fire department arrives. However, there are some situations that must be considered. First, in many situations, it would be far better to have an occupant of the building take action with an extinguisher during the incipient stage of a fire. This may extinguish the fire, thus reducing damage and threat to life. At least, the fire would be held in check until trained firefighters could take over.

The selection of Option 2 creates a situation where only selected employees are trained to use extinguishers and authorized to fight a fire. Although this option provides for both the evacuation of the majority of employees and some level of incipient fire attack, there is always the potential that an untrained occupant may be the first to confront or be trapped by a fire and may lack the skills to take appropriate action. Certainly, many factors must be taken into consideration before determining which option to select. The choice should be made after examining the hazards of the workplace involved, the response and capability of the local fire department, and the capability of the employees/occupants. Note that the employer must select one of the options. Failing to do so often will result in a citation and fines from OSHA for failing to meet its minimum requirements. OSHA has taken these actions many times and has even imprisoned employers who failed to train their employees and develop fire safety and evacuation procedures.

Although some in the fire service may oppose these requirements, the employer has no option under federal law....

For this discussion, I have avoided the obvious question of occupancy classification. The majority of high-rise buildings may encompass multiple occupancy concerns including those of assembly, mercantile, and residential/lodging issues.

Diverse safety concerns

In the weeks following the events of September 11, I encountered two very different attitudes related to high-rise safety. Owners and managers of high-rise buildings in places like New York and other major cities have had increased concerns about high-rise safety and evacuation training. In many other parts of the country, however, little has changed. By contrast, terrorism, a far less likely potential in most metropolitan areas, is receiving far more attention than necessary. High-rise occupants are more likely to encounter fires and other "nonterrorist" events that would present safety concerns.

Mail handling is being given excessive attention in many situations. Many more deaths will be caused by fire, and even the flu this year, than will be caused by contacting anthrax through the mail system. Yet, there is greater concern in the anthrax area, and the business sector is capitalizing on this.

Add the notion that "it couldn't happen here" to the general lack of understanding the requirements for evacuation training, and it becomes clear that these issues will not be properly addressed on their own. The fact remains that the majority of occupants in high-rise buildings may not have received any training in fire safety and evacuation or may have chosen not to participate when training was given, despite the fact that such training has been a requirement for more than 30 years. From the perspective of the occupants, there is great concern for personal safety. They want to be trained on what to do in an emergency. There is also greater apprehension about working in high-rise buildings.

The main reason for the lack of training is that the "Operating Features" section(s) of the *Life Safety Code®* is not being enforced in many areas. High-rise building owners and management are not being required to comply by providing this training. The legal issues and fines for not doing so bring some accountability for not meeting these requirements, but the fact remains that these actions are taken after lives have been lost.

The proposed solution

In the majority of fire departments across our nation, there are insufficient personnel and resources to provide training assistance to meet these requirements. The only viable solution is private sector resources that can assist in the training. In addition to the basic requirements in the occupancy-specific chapters of the *Life Safety Code®*, there is the need to use performance-based options. One such tool well suited for addressing life safety concerns is the "Life Safety Evaluation." A detailed review of this process would require an entire article, but the existence of this evaluation method should be recognized here. The "Life Safety Evaluation" is intended mainly for assembly occupancies; however, it can be applied to any situation. The code also permits the evaluation to be performed by persons "acceptable to the Authority Having Jurisdiction," minimizing the potential additional demand on public fire and life safety services.

The only way that the required evaluation and training will be completed is through enforcement of these requirements. In some jurisdictions, enforcement has not been pursued because of a lack of resources. It is interesting that these requirements are set aside or simply ignored because of a lack of resources to implement them when this is not the case for other "building"-related requirements.

Management-related issues are of equal or greater concern. Building owners and managers must be held accountable for meeting the safety training requirements for assembly, business, residential, correctional, mercantile, industrial, and health-care occupancies.

Firefighting demands

Finally, there is the issue of fire personnel waging battle against high-rise fires. No examination of these issues would be complete without addressing the fact that all our prevention and training will not ensure that fires and other emergencies will not occur. As noted, our tradition has been to load individual firefighters with hoses, air packs, hand tools, and other equipment; send them up 20, 30, 50, or 100 flights of stairs; and then have them initiate fire attack and assist with evacuation. It is almost unimaginable that we would expect firefighters to traverse such a great height, let alone with lots of equipment.

If we are to continue to occupy and have fires in "mega high-rises," then we must rethink our expectations pertaining to firefighting personnel and how they access these buildings. Clearly, it is impractical to expect firefighters to carry such heavy loads of equipment. But beyond this, at what height is it impractical to expect firefighters to take themselves higher and higher by stairs alone?

We must examine better methods for getting firefighters to the upper floors more quickly and safely. We should expect building owners to provide for the storage of firefighting tools and equipment on upper floors of high-rise buildings—equipment storage and maintenance under the control of the fire department with the cost defrayed by the high-rise building owner. In some places in California, upper floors of high-rise buildings have been equipped with air bottle filling stations. This is a start, but more must be done. The only practical approach is to ensure that firefighters can access upper floors and be properly equipped in the process without undue demands. Elevators have been off limits during building fires. Is there a solution in bringing back the "dumbwaiter" and having an equipment-only lift in high-rise buildings? Or would it be more practical to construct hardened elevator shafts and equipment that could be used reliably in emergency situations?

Perhaps this selection has raised more issues than it has solved, but the hope is that you at least have been challenged to rethink high-rise safety. We must reexamine our definition of high-rise. We must look at additional requirements for "mega high-rise" buildings. Collectively, through our code-making process, we can develop changes that will improve high-rise safety. Until then, we must ensure that existing requirements are properly enforced. I am reminded here of one definition of insanity: "doing the same things over and over again, but expecting different results." Let's do things differently, and better. Through better enforcement, education, preparation, and response, we can expect to achieve the goal of greater safety for high-rise building occupants and those sent to fight fires in them.

References

Brannigan, Francis L. *Building Construction for the Fire Service*. Quincy Mass.: National Fire Protection Association, 1971.

Colonna, Gyr R., ed. *Introduction to Employee Fire and Life Safety*. Quincy Mass.: National Fire Protection Association, 2001.

DiNenno, Philip J., Craig L. Beyler, Richard L. P. Custer et al., eds. *The SFPE Handbook of Fire Protection Engineering*. Published in 1995 by the National Fire Protection Association in Quincy, Mass., and the Society of Fire Protection Engineers in Bethesda, Md.

Faith, Nicholas. *Blaze: The Forensics of Fire*. London: Channel 4 Books, 1999.

O'Hagen, John T. *High Rise Fire and Life Safety*. Fair Lawn, N.J.: Fire Engineering, 1977.

Part IV

Response

14 Public works personnel as first responders

Janet Ward

Certain events—Pearl Harbor, the Kennedy Assassination, the Challenger disaster—become the defining points for a generation, the one event for which everyone in that generation will say, "This is where I was when I heard."

The Sept. 11, 2001, attacks on the World Trade Center and the Pentagon were such a defining point. But for Peter King, they had a double significance. King, executive director of the Kansas City, Mo.–based American Public Works Association (APWA), was in Philadelphia at that organization's annual conference when the planes hit.

He and the 26,000 members of APWA immediately grasped that neither the country nor the public works community would ever be the same. "There was talk of shutting down the conference," King says. "The decision was to continue. We immediately convened the board of directors and the emergency management committee. It couldn't have been a better group of people to have together at that time. All of them were public works directors trained in emergency response."

APWA moved quickly to address the Sept. 11 attacks. By the time Philadelphia's hotels began rolling out the tv screens to allow their visitors to follow the events, the APWA leadership was calling together its forces. The group met with convention center security personnel and began putting together a communications center to allow its members to contact their communities. The board of directors and the emergency management committee agreed to meet hourly to assess the situation and discuss strategy.

Blue-collar first responders

But what was fortunate for King presented problems for cities and counties across the country. Once the reality of the attacks settled in, communities began to panic. For many of them, the heart and soul of their public works departments were in Philadelphia, with no way to get home once the nation's air transportation system had shut down.

A number of those cities and counties actually footed the bill for their public works directors to purchase vans and cars so they could drive home. Many communities began to doubt the wisdom of having so many of their critical personnel away from home at one time. It was a time of validation for the public works community, though that validation has worn thin in the subsequent months.

Some 20 years before the Sept. 11 attacks, the Federal Emergency Management Agency had developed the policies and procedures that would form the basis of its terrorism response guidelines. In developing those policies, FEMA targeted what it defined as "first responders," police and law enforcement, public health, fire and public works personnel.

Since Sept. 11, the term "first responder" has gained a cachet that no one could have predicted. New York's fire and police departments have become the nation's new heroes, and, as a result of the anthrax scares later that fall, reams of paper have been devoted

Originally published as "Public Works: The Nation's Forgotten First Responders," *Homeland Protection Professional*, Vol. 1, No. 1, pages 36–39, July/August, 2002. Published by A. J. Parrino & Associates, Western Springs, Illinois. Reprinted with permission of the publisher.

to the critical importance of the country's public health system. And public works? Well, public works has become the forgotten first responders.

It's a role that, while not exactly relished, is accepted by public works professionals around the country. "They're the ones who handle the rescues," says Paul Brum. "We serve in a support role. We're the ones who set up the barricades and make sure the Porta-Potties work."

As Oklahoma City's longtime public works director, Brum has some experience with the issue. His office was a critical component in recovery efforts after the 1995 bombing of the Alfred P. Murrah Federal Building. "They're the people in the white hats," he says of the police and fire personnel. "We're the blue-collar workers. We accept that."

National Emergency Response and Rescue Training Center

However, while most public works employees have no problem accepting their support role, many think that role is rarely fully appreciated. First-response training programs abound, but they are often geared to public safety and health professionals, despite the fact that much of the information imparted is critical to the operation of public works in the wake of an emergency. The one program specifically designed to train public works professionals to respond to Sept. 11-like crises is relatively new.

The National Emergency Response and Rescue Training Center (NERRTC), operated out of Texas A&M University's Texas Engineering Extension Service, offers counterterrorism training at its College Station headquarters directed at public works departments throughout the country.[1] Additionally, the center funds on-site training free to any city or county public works department that requests it. Since Sept. 11, calls to the center have mushroomed. "We used to do one course a week, now we're doing three to four," says Mark McCain, principal consultant with St. Helena Island, S.C.–based Public Works Emergency Management Services and an NERRTC instructor.

The center's three-day courses are based on eight modules, which vary in length. The first module covers an introduction to weapons of mass destruction and encompasses the motives for their use and the types of actions that might be expected. Modules on legal issues, vunerability assessment, incident command, resource management, incident response, recovery and plan development follow.

By the summer of 2002, the center had trained between 1,600 and 1,700 people in some 55 communities. Its integrated approach—it is designed for public works personnel, but all first responders are welcomed—is what sets the program apart.

"We did a training exercise in St. Croix," says Roy Robinson, an NERRTC course manager. "Ron Hatcher, the training officer for the Virgin Islands Police Department, said it was the first time everyone had been at the same table. That's pretty much the message we hear. We try to engage the other folks—fire, law enforcement, hazmat, emergency medical, public health—because we want an integrated response. It can seem strange for some people, because they're not used to having public works people involved."

"I recommend it very, very strongly," says Phil Chin, assistant to the public works director for the City and County of San Francisco, which just completed the training. "It helped us focus on the effects of terrorism. We have a fairly good handle on natural disasters, but we weren't too knowledgeable about the specifics of terrorism or WMD. An earthquake is fairly non-discriminating. Terrorism is focused. We learned what to look for and what to look at."

Other training opportunities

Besides the NERRTC, three of the best training programs, the Center for National Response in Kanawha County, W.Va.; the Center for Domestic Preparedness in Anniston, Ala.; and FEMA's Emergency Management Institute in Emmitsburg, Md., offer a number of tracks that cover functions generally considered part of the public works bailiwick: hazmat response, mass transit episodes and multi-hazard building design.

The Center for National Response

The Center for National Response operates out of Memorial Tunnel, an abandoned turnpike tunnel in southern West Virginia.[2] Operated by Titan Systems Corp.'s Defense Programs Division and financed by the National Guard Bureau of the Department of Defense, the center provides training to federal, state and local emergency teams.

Intriguingly, the center has no defined curriculum; the staff creates response situations designed for whatever kind of group is currently taking its training. The center has designed scenarios ranging from production of biological toxins to subway derailments to accidents involving over-the-road toxic cargo. Cameras record response actions from start to finish, giving participants a take-home record of the training.

The Center for Domestic Preparedness

Located at the former Fort McClellan (Ala.) army base, the Center for Domestic Preparedness is the product of a congressional directive to create a site that would "serve as a training facility for all relevant federally supported training efforts that target state and local law enforcement, firefighters, emergency medical personnel and other key agencies such as public works."[3] It has offered courses in dealing with WMD response, with concentrations in technical and hazmat response and incident command.

The Emergency Management Institute

FEMA's Emergency Management Institute has been popular with a number of public works departments, including Oklahoma City's.[4] Its Integrated Emergency Management course is a four-and-a-half day "exercise-based training activity" primarily aimed at elected and appointed local government officials. Some versions of the course involve events in generic communities, and some target specific communities.

Training at all three centers is free; transportation and lodging are picked up by the participants. "If you're not going through a training process at least every two years, you will miss something," says Oklahoma City's Brum.

"The mop-up guys"

Getting public works professionals to these centers has not been easy. People who run the country's water and wastewater plants—who fill its potholes, repair its bridges and wear overalls to work—tend not to see themselves as occupying the rarefied strata that include traditional first responders.

That surprises some people, like Paula Gordon, director of special projects of the research program in social and organizational learning at George Washington University. Gordon, who wrote "Infrastructure Threats and Challenges: Before and After September 11, 2001" for the American Society for Public Administration, posits that part of the problem may be a lack of public relations savvy within the public works community. "They're just not good at tooting their own horn."

Larry Lux agrees. "Generally speaking, the public works community needs to become more involved in the political process," he says. "We need to take stronger and more affirmative advocacy positions, both locally and on the Hill. It's the only way our voices will be recognized. I've made a career out of [trying to get attention for public works], but I'm only one voice. We need thousands of voices."

Lux, president of Plainfield, Ill.–based Lux Advisors, which counsels communities on emergency and disaster management, is a member of APWA's Emergency Management Board and an adjunct faculty instructor at FEMA's Emergency Management Institute. He calls public works employees "the mop-up guys."

"People are absolutely unaware of the importance of public works" in homeland protection, Lux says. "Public works is not thought of as a first responder. What we do isn't glamorous. Fire and law enforcement people arrive in big red vehicles with their sirens going. After they're finished, public works comes up in their little yellow trucks."

Lux insists that communities need to more seriously pursue homeland protection training opportunities for their public works employees. "Not much in that regard has changed since Sept. 11," he says. "The government is earmarking a lot of money for homeland security, but none of the language and none of the money is targeted at improving public works response and training."

In fact, although public works was never mentioned, the Heritage Foundation, a conservative Washington, D.C., think tank, seemed to target the profession in a backgrounder called "Meeting the Needs of America's First Responders. "From 1996 to 1999, the federal government was able to provide [WMD] response training to only 134,000 of the nation's 9 million first responders," the paper noted. It cited the problems of inadequate information regarding available training programs, expensive and inconvenient programs and lack of coordination as issues that the federal government must address.

Fighting an out-of-date image

"Part of the problem," Gordon says, "is how 'homeland protection' is being defined. We need to expand the definition."

To some extent, that is happening. Dust from the World Trade Center still hung in the air as national concern over the safety of the country's water plants, highways and bridges was being ratcheted up.

Much of the early homeland security legislation focused on securing the nation's water supply and other "critical infrastructure." Additionally, in a March 2002 letter to APWA members, FEMA Director Joe Allbaugh noted that "at this time, perhaps more than at any other time, we realize the importance of public works infrastructure, facilities and services."

FEMA and APWA are ironing out the details of a Memorandum of Understanding that will provide the basis for a new cooperative effort between the two groups. And APWA has been active in providing comments on proposed legislation and on budget items, according to Karen Bloodworth, manager of professional development programs for the organization.

Still, Bloodworth concedes that pr is a big part of the problem in APWA's efforts to put the importance of public works on the homeland defense agenda. "We haven't been that good at [public relations]," she says. "The staff agrees that PR has been a shortcoming. We are making an effort to change that."

Bloodworth points out that public works functions in emergency management are all-encompassing and include engineering, health and safety codes, roads and bridges, dams, canals, wastewater collection and treatment, electric generation and distribution, telephone service, garbage collection, debris removal and flood control. "Public works people are so involved in the whole emergency management process," says Gordon. "It's hard to fathom how they can be overlooked."

"When a disaster occurs, the first people in are law enforcement, fire and medical personnel," Lux says. "After a time, it's all public works. The cleanup and restoration of the community is almost 100% public works. We are critical to first response. We need to make everyone understand that."

Notes

1. For information on the National Response and Rescue Training Center, see http://teexweb.tamu.edu/division.cfm?div=NEERRTC.
2. For information on the Center for National Response, see www.wvmemorialtunnel.com.
3. For information on the Center for Domestic Preparedness, see www.ojp.usdoj.gov/odp.
4. For information on the Emergency Management Institute of the Federal Emergency Management Agency, see http://training.fema.gov.

15 Automated public notification systems

Gary Raymer and Rick Wimberly

Automated notification systems, formerly considered an expensive luxury for larger urban agencies, are now becoming standard equipment for police departments and public safety organizations of all sizes. No longer do first responders need to rely on time-consuming and labor-intensive phone trees, which often fail to deliver detailed and useful information during emergency situations. Moreover, manual phone trees limit the number of participating agencies in the call lineup, narrowing notification and response capabilities.

In the wake of September 11, 2001, high-speed notification systems also are used more frequently for nonemergency communications. They can serve as a community outreach tool, ensuring better communication with business and residents. And the systems can be used with neighboring agencies to ensure a seamless approach on country-wide or regional levels.

When such systems were still relatively new to smaller law enforcement agencies, Kentucky's Bowling Green Police Department—which currently has 96 sworn officers—acquired an automated high-speed notification systems. The department found that activation was as simple as placing a phone call or pushing a computer key and that notification times in emergency situations were significantly shortened. The department also discovered that the systems could be used for numerous proactive police and community notifications involving schools, hospitals, nursing homes, banks and pharmacies.

Police departments across the regions, as well as state and federal agencies, also tapped into the Bowling Green Police Department's system for true cross-jurisdictional use. Sharing costs among participating agencies, the department reduced its own expenses yet became an essential informational hub for the region. The department now receives numerous invitations to share information about its experience and expertise in the implementation of this technology. This selection provides an overview of one department's use of its high-speed notification technology in a cross-jurisdictional setting.

The setting

The city of Bowling Green is located along Interstate 65 in southern Kentucky, approximately 100 miles south of Louisville and 65 miles north of Nashville, Tennessee. With a resident population of 50,000, Bowling Green is a metropolitan hub for a predominantly rural surrounding area.

The city draws 200,000 commuters daily for recreation, employment, and healthcare. Students and faculty at Western Kentucky University make up 16,000 of those commuters. Interstate 65, a major north-south corridor, intersects the city, as does the

Originally published as "Obtaining and Using High-Speed Notification Technology in a Cross-Jurisdictional Setting." Reprinted from *The Police Chief*, Vol. LXIX, No. 6, pages 38–41, June, 2002. Copyright held by the International Association of Chiefs of Police, 515 North Washington Street, Alexandria, VA 22314 USA. Further reproduction without express written permission from IACP is strictly prohibited.

L&N railroad—both known to carry heavy commercial traffic with subsequent spill hazards.

The area is routinely plagued by severe weather, as it lies in a tornado-prone region of the southeast. Moreover, Bowling Green is home to 36 hazmat sites, including GM's Corvette manufacturing plant and Holley Automotive, maker of racecar carburetors and fuel injection systems.

The shortcomings of a traditional notification system

In 1976 the Bowling Green Police Department created a neighborhood watch program, which now involves about 70 watch groups. The program relied on manual call trees to alert its top members who, in turn, made calls to the other participants. Call-outs included those about lost children, burglary suspects, as well as man-made and natural disasters.

The manual call trees caused uncertainty when group members needed to relay updated information. Apart from quarterly face-to-face meetings and occasional alerts, no regular communication channels existed to check the status of the neighborhood watch groups. Additionally, team recalls and police call-outs were performed manually, generating concern about response time, the conveying of incident-specific information or potentially life-saving instruction.

To address these community concerns, a crime prevention officer of the Bowling Green Police Department began looking for a way to improve the neighborhood watch program, to provide for immediate relay of information to the participants. High-speed notification technology was determined to be the best solution for fast, accurate communication to enhance community policing efforts, as well as to ensure the quick response of department personnel.

Evaluation of systems

In early 1997 the police department evaluated several high-speed notification systems in search of one that could meet the growing demands of both the department and the community. The department required a solution that could provide automation of all emergency and nonemergency communication procedures with immediate verification of call receipt.

The research found that while some providers offered a basic notification system with limited or expensive add-on features, other companies had the ability to modify their technology to meet the department's site-specific needs, as well as those of the surrounding communities. Equally important to department officials preparing to purchase this technology was the providing company's references, commitment to customer support, and dedication to regular system upgrades.

With high-speed notification technology fast becoming an essential component of both routine and emergency communications for law enforcement, the department was more easily able to secure funding through a grant from the U.S. Department of Justice. The Bowling Green Police Department received competitive bids from three providers. The agency preferred the Microsoft Windows operating system, so that ruled out companies that used DOS-based technology.

The department ultimately purchased the software and hardware for a high-speed notification system and geographic information system (GIS) mapping interface. Additional costs included minimal support fees, software upgrades, and the installation of additional phone lines.

Planning

With the grant in hand in October, and the installation of the new system planned for December 1997, the department did the necessary groundwork for pre-implementation. Recognizing that the department's 15 dispatchers were already working under an existing operational system, planners decided that the new equipment would be housed in the crime prevention office. This location would provide dispatchers physical or remote access during system training. As part of the training process, scenarios for possible call-out situations were created.

Survey forms, easily modified for basic roster information such as phone numbers and other personnel data, were created. The department used these forms to survey its police force, as well as neighborhood watch groups, fire departments, banks, emergency medical services and others. As the integration of the high-speed notification technology began, the department created a time-line and implementation plan. The department described the plan as "crawl, walk, and run."

Implementation

Within the timeline and implementation plan, basic system functions were identified and established. Initially a severe weather threat scenario was created. The original phone tree contact list had 33 people on it. The new system permitted an expansion to 147, adding key contacts such as schools, utility companies, other law enforcement agencies, day care centers, hospitals, and even the media.

Satisfied with the results, the department created numerous call-out scenarios and included other agencies in the communications plan. Allowed to access the equipment, these agencies quickly determined that they could enhance their own emergency notifications using the notification system.

System details

The Bowling Green Police Department employs the following scenario templates for the timely, accurate delivery of information:

- Simple delivery—all participants called and information conveyed
- Simple delivery with response—all participants called and their response(s) entered through touch-tone phone dialing
- Secure delivery—all participants called and information given upon entry of a valid identification code
- Secure delivery with response—all participants called, information delivered upon entry of a valid identification code, and their responses logged through touch-tone phone.

Uses

The first real test of the system came when a tornado roared through Arkansas, Tennessee, and Kentucky, causing widespread damage in the Bowling Green area. With the police department received word of a tornado that touch down in south Warren County, it quickly alerted other local law enforcement agencies, the National Weather Service, hospitals, schools, daycare centers, and the media. Each party was notified twice in less than nine minutes. While softball-sized hail damaged 11,000 roofs and pounded 3,000 cars, personal injuries were kept to a minimum because of the advance notice of the approaching storm front.

The Bowling Green Police Department also routinely uses the notification system to cut down on criminal activity. Located near the Tennessee state line, Bowling Green is a prime target for criminals who prey upon the city and then flee back across the border. One perpetrator, a woman from Murfreesboro, Tennessee, attracted the attention of bank officials after attempting to open the account with a suspicious $14,800 check. When the transaction was questioned, she abruptly left the bank and went to another.

The bank notified police, who used the system to send out an alert. A third bank called within a minute to report that the woman was in its lobby. Police officers quickly apprehended the woman, who was in possession of eight counterfeit checks and had planned to open accounts in various banks, withdraw cash, and flee with the money.

The system was also used to locate and capture a Tennessee woman who had stolen prescription pads and was attempting to purchase drugs from Bowling Green pharmacies.

By issuing alerts and warnings, the department is able to quickly apprehend crime suspects and ensure public safety during emergencies. Companies victimized by crime receive subsequent notifications, relaying the police department's progress in ongoing investigations. The system is also used to alert other businesses in the affected area, enabling them to take necessary precautions against such criminal activity.

Using the system across jurisdictions

The Bowling Green Police Department has allowed the other departments and agencies, including those outside Warren County, to send their own alerts through Bowling Green's notification system or to activate many of the more than 100 scenarios created since the late 1990s.

The privately owned emergency medical service (EMS) in Bowling Green uses the notification system to call off-duty ambulance personnel. The Bowling Green Fire Department, the Emergency Operations Center, area schools, and the regional jail also use the system to send out a variety of alerts. The multijurisdictional I-65 Drug Interdiction Taskforce, and law enforcement agencies along the 145-mile stretch between Nashville and Louisville, use the system to stop drug trafficking.

Most recently, the U.S. Attorney's Office for the Western District of Kentucky set up an antiterrorist taskforce after September 11, to include the Bowling Green Police Department as well as federal, state, and local law enforcement agencies. After U.S. Attorney General John Ashcroft suggested the creation of phone trees for various regional taskforces, the Bowling Green Police Department took the next step and automated its own taskforce notifications. During a test in March 2002, more than 90 taskforce members were contacted within six minutes. Like EMS, the antiterrorist taskforce can activate the system remotely by touchtone phone, putting the call-out into immediate action.

Figure 15-1.
City of Bowling Green police department recommendations: High-speed notification systems.

The Bowling Green Police Department recommends that other departments contemplating implementation of a high-speed notification system take the following steps to ensure smooth installation and operation:

Before implementation

- Ensure that top managers and commanders are fully committed to the project.
- Size up the environment early by identifying and understanding the unique aspects of the technology and what success it can create.
- Determine constraints and areas of conflict and deal with all present contradictions by creating a shared need.
- Consider rapid-implementation with multiple project phases. Simple scenarios and smaller groups are a great way to start.
- For best results, start training within the department before the start of on-site implementation.

During implementation

- Use basic system functions quickly to ensure rapid success for buy-in from both the department and the community.
- Model the results of successful scenarios by replicating call-flows in similar situations.
- Use the system to address the needs of those requiring public safety and crime-prevention information on the front end.

With several users having secure access to the system, priority levels must be assigned to the various notifications. When nonemergency scenarios are running, they can be automatically paused to allow emergency alerts and notifications to take precedence. The nonemergency scenarios automatically resume upon call-out completion. All of these notifications can be accommodated under the system's default settings or set manually as needed.

The Bowling Green Police Department further tested the system's capabilities by creating a mock disaster, with five different emergency scenarios successfully running at the same time.

High-speed notification technology has clearly demonstrated its relevance as an effective communications tool, enabling law enforcement to quickly and accurately connect with other agencies, counties and communities-at-risk. Such technology warrants serious consideration for agencies striving toward optimization of resources, effective information flow and management at all levels. A high-speed notification system can be a very powerful tool for law enforcement, allowing department personnel to work smarter, not harder.

16 | Geographic information systems: Mapping the response

Russ Johnson

Prior to Sept. 11, 2001, geographic information systems (GIS) were typically thought of simply as mapping tools, useful for plotting out utility systems, watersheds, population densities, vegetation and the other systems that make up a geographic area. That has all changed.

From the first moments of the attacks on the World Trade Center (WTC) and the Pentagon, and through the days, weeks and months afterwards, GIS played a vital role in emergency coordination and operations. Combined with data integration and people and resource organization, GIS has helped numerous agencies assisting in the response efforts. Now, as the emergency response community prepares for potential future attacks, GIS will continue to play a vital role, not only in responding to events, but in planning and preparation.

Mapping the response

Almost immediately after the attacks on New York, a mapping center was established within then-mayor Rudy Giuliani's Office of Emergency Management (OEM). The center was equipped with 20 GIS workstations and five mapmaking plotters.

Because New York had long used GIS, the city already had a rich geographic database that included maps and digital imagery of its critical infrastructure. That database provided a foundation for the OEM's GIS efforts, which, in turn, provided a foundation for a number of recovery activities.

What emerged from the OEM's efforts was a database enterprise for storing, managing and editing spatial and related tabular information, which allowed for disparate information pools created independently by private and public utilities, fire, public works, water, sewer, police and other agencies to be integrated and stored in one location. The centralized environment provided dynamic mapping capabilities that spurred optimized emergency field operations.

The OEM created a storehouse of geographic data, including maps that charted:

- transportation and public access
- major river crossings
- subway service
- telephone usage
- pedestrian and vehicular traffic restrictions
- power grids
- operational areas

Originally published as "GIS at the WTC," *Homeland Protection Professional*, Vol. 1, No. 1, pages 32–35, July/August, 2002. Published by A. J. Parrino & Associates, Western Springs, Illinois. Reprinted with permission of the publisher.

- damage assessments
- fire, emergency services and police emergency response assets
- staging areas
- water outages
- personnel services, such as food and water stations.

The office also created three-dimensional maps of affected buildings. All told, the mapping services team produced thousands of maps.

Maps and operations

Those maps were used during daily briefings and for mapping incident action plans that involved breaking sections of Ground Zero into functional units using maps and grids. Using the maps, Urban Search and Rescue teams were assigned to grid sectors each day.

Once a grid sector was searched, information resulting from the search was entered into the database. Recorded information was linked to grid cells.

After a grid cell was thoroughly examined, crane operators carefully removed a layer of debris, which was loaded into trucks and taken to an examination area. The debris was spread out to allow for precise inspection and then marked and recorded so that anything found could be mapped and linked to its grid cell location at the WTC.

As floors were examined and surveyed, voids, or open pockets among debris wreckage, were mapped using GIS. Color-coded maps of building levels revealed the status of the search operations for the floor. For example, color maps revealed whether sections had been searched and cleared, had collapsed, or were flooded or exposed to a hazard such as fire or potentially toxic pollutants.

Aerial photos were overlaid with square grids and mapped to provide a continuous time-stamp monitor for operations. Maps could then be examined to evaluate operations progress. In addition, detailed ground-level photos were hot-linked to the GIS database map so users could select a building or grid cell on the base map and quickly access it.

Asset and infrastructure maps generated before the attacks allowed users to more quickly locate items after the attack by providing reference points in areas where rubble and debris were disorienting for response workers. Maps of floor plans and other assets allowed workers to find items such as downed electric lines, gas mains that needed to be examined for leaks, or other critical infrastructure assets.

Emergency responders also used light-intensity detection and ranging (LIDAR) images to create three-dimensional maps illustrating smoldering hotspots, voids and pile movement. LIDAR images were produced daily to provide information on activities such as debris shift and fire progression.

Networked maps

Beyond mapping, emergency responders used an online intranet application called E-Team, which allowed different agencies to share and update information via the Web and to keep each other apprised of their activities. The application was designed to provide GIS functionality to people without GIS experience.

While the GIS map professionals generated back-end computer mapping capabilities and high-quality maps, E-Team allowed emergency response workers to work with information from their desktops and view an overall map of the incident that was updated as events evolved. An E-Team user simply called up a map with color-coded icons and symbols and then clicked on an icon to get information concerning fieldwork status, background, resources, agencies involved and other relevant activity information.

Emergency decision support

Additionally, GIS helped crews locating power lines, telephone and water service; utility infrastructure generators; bridges that would support heavy load removal; and fuel tanks, and it provided them with building ownership information. Deploying emergency personnel, routing crews, identifying larger open areas in lower Manhattan for staging equipment (cranes, for example) and assigning areas of work were made easier with digital maps. As more information was collected and stored in the GIS, advanced modeling features helped staff model the collapse of buildings and how the debris was scattered.

Health officials also used GIS to map air plumes in order to track asbestos, PCBs and other toxic materials.

In addition, GIS helped the city get information to the public. Maps enhanced news stories by providing visual information related to recovery efforts, giving readers a view of the events as they transpired.

Mapping the future

Obviously, GIS is useful in rescue and recovery efforts. However, GIS could be even more critical in surveillance, preparation, planning and mitigation. Surveillance and detection of potential terrorist activity is crucial in preventing future attacks.

Like any criminal activity, terrorism requires funding, people, materials and logistics, and the connections between those involve patterns in time and space. GIS techniques can be used to correlate apparently disconnected events, letting the big picture emerge from huge volumes of data.

The key is the fusion of data from disparate sources into a common spatial framework. As a growing range of sensors is deployed to gather information concerning suspicious activities, GIS can be used to integrate the resulting information into a meaningful picture.

Assessing and analyzing the locations and vulnerabilities of water supplies, roads, bridges, distribution pipelines, public transportation, populations, schools, hazardous materials, public assemblies, national monuments and other assets can be performed efficiently using GIS. When vulnerabilities are identified, GIS can help identify mitigation strategies and can model various alternatives, including setbacks around buildings, closing certain access points, fencing exposed areas and relocating hazardous materials.

GIS supports other critical homeland security planning requirements, including determining evacuation routes, locations and capacities of evacuation shelters, and potential locations of staging areas, incident management facilities and public safety response assets.

The chaos and confusion created during major emergencies can be more effectively managed when responders and workers have a clear picture of what needs to be done and where it needs to be done. In complex emergency events, many people from different agencies must respond and take coordinated actions, which are usually communicated through the medium of a map.

GIS not only provides maps; it also provides great amounts of additional information about each feature on the map. And though it's a powerful asset in the response and recovery toolbox, its greatest promise may be in helping to prevent future 9–11s.

17 | Dispatch center services

Randall D. Larson

There was a lot of attention paid to the challenges and tragedies that faced our first responders on Sept. 11, 2001, but very little attention was given to the dispatchers who worked diligently and consistently behind the scenes. In many instances, they were the last to hear the voices of civilians trapped in the World Trade Center, calling from cell phones on hijacked airliners, and the rescuers who were lost in the collapse of the towers.

When the Department of Justice developed the Domestic Preparedness Program in 1998, it made sure to include 911 dispatchers in that training. This made sense, recognizing that our nation's emergency telecommunicators are the ones who will most likely receive the first notice of a terrorist or weapons of mass destruction (WMD) event, and they are the ones who will be at the center of coordinating and integrating the response to ongoing homeland security concerns.

"America's 911 communications personnel represent the *first* first responder to each and every type of emergency situation imaginable," says Robert Martin, executive director of the National Academies of Emergency Dispatch. "Not only can good information in the 911 dispatch center help to spot early patterns or warning signs of possible terrorist activities, but properly trained and certified dispatchers can also provide immediate assistance in the way of giving practical advice to callers."

With the encouragement of Attorney General Ashcroft and the Bush Administration, Neighborhood Watch organizations are beginning to proliferate, undoubtedly resulting in an increase in calls to local 911 centers.

"Seeing a lot of our national figureheads including our President directing people to call 911 when they feel something is suspicious, it's obvious that we are America's first-line phone call," says Kevin Willett, senior instructor for Public Safety Training Consultants, a national trainer of 911 dispatchers. "We have to be prepared and we have to know where to refer calls and how to handle them appropriately."

"It's important that the dispatcher is well trained to pick up the clues that will indicate that this is an event that might have much greater consequences to the community, whether it's terrorism caused or not," adds Dr. Frances Edwards-Winslow, director of the San Jose (Calif.) Office of Emergency Services.

In February 2002, the Association of Public Safety Communications Officials–International (APCO) launched a Homeland Security Task Force in response to the demands placed on public safety communications in the aftermath of Sept. 11. The Task Force identified six critical homeland security issues demanding primary attention by dispatch centers:

1) **Security** for dispatch centers, communications systems, and infrastructure.

2) **Survivability and redundancy** of dispatch centers and communications systems.

3) **Interoperability** of radio systems.

Originally published as "It Starts in Dispatch," *Homeland Protection Professional*, Vol. 1, No. 1, pages 43–47, July/August, 2002. Published by A. J. Parrino & Associates, Western Springs, Illinois. Reprinted with permission of the publisher.

4) **Impact of public safety operations** on communications centers. How does the response to major incidents impact dispatch operations?

5) Focus on **training** and the needs of telecommunicators/dispatchers.

6) Focus on **equipment and infrastructure**. How can dispatch centers partner with the private sector to create better technology?

APCO also hopes to increase awareness about the funding needs of local 911 and communication centers. "It is hoped that the information gathered will be of assistance not only in regards to homeland security, but also as a means of improving the reliability of day-to-day operations," says Barry Furey, communications director for Knox County, Tenn., and chair of the APCO Homeland Security Task Force.

Communications center security

911 and dispatch administrators need to look carefully at their own premise security to ensure they aren't susceptible to sabotage or intrusion. Maintaining a dispatch center's security and survivability in the event of an attack is paramount to a response agency's ability to respond against terrorism.

The University of Wisconsin at Madison, for example, put a live security camera on the building's air intake and ordered a supply of gas masks as a contingency against a chemical attack on the facility.

Other centers have also stockpiled supplies and beefed up security measures. "Dispatch agencies need to be secure not only against terrorism, but also for more conventional kinds of criminal activity," says Tony Harrison, a dispatch instructor with The Public Safety Group. "I know several dispatch centers that could be taken out of order with a single pipe bomb, because all the phone lines enter the facility at one location and the phone box is above ground."

The Columbia 9-1-1 Communications District in St. Helens, Ore., recently revised its facility security policy. The central administrative area is no longer open to the public during business hours, and all entry is screened by on-duty personnel. Additional external cameras and monitors were installed, as well as expanded capacity to monitor those camera views.

"We are no longer offering tours and visits from the public," explains Sally J. Jones, the district's administrator. "Our physical address was removed from our Web site, and only our Post Office Box is published now. As an agency, we also participated in developing a statewide procedure for handling homeland security messages distribution."

Redundancy is also a necessity, especially for facilities as vital as communications centers. Yet budgets rarely allow such a major expense as a back-up facility, especially one that, in the eyes of local politicians, might never be used.

Nonetheless, there are solutions. For example, Milwaukee's communications director came up with a way to justify developing a back-up 911 site by setting it up as a primary dispatch training site. The equipment is constantly being used and therefore tested, and it gets 911 trainers off-site and able to train hands-on without being on top of the people actually working. Partnering with neighboring agencies to be each other's back-up call receipt and dispatch site is another way to accommodate redundancy on limited budgets.

Interoperability

The ability to communicate not only with your own resources but also with those of your neighboring agencies will also be vital during any homeland security plan. If a WMD or terrorist event does happen in your community, you'll most likely require the assistance of neighboring jurisdictions to mitigate the incident, not to mention the federal responders that will begin swarming in.

Speaking to the Senate Communications Subcommittee on March 6, 2002, APCO president Glen Nash reminded Congress that, especially with the new homeland security responsibilities being placed on state and local public safety agencies, "the need for effective radio communications is heightened even more …" and that "there will be even greater demand for public safety [radio] spectrum." What is needed are adequate radio channels with adequate radio coverage, including a combined approach with interoperability between all public safety agencies and support entities. Solutions can be costly and long-term, but must be thought out now. At the same time, workable solutions can be found through short-term means.

A report on public safety communications during the attack on the Pentagon, issued in February 2002 by the Public Safety Wireless Network, concluded that, to link agencies during a major incident, planning, training and asset management are more urgently needed than sophisticated technology. The group noted that at the Pentagon, a lack of sops, politics, and turf battles prevented the implementation of available technical solutions.

How agencies communicate, and the daily habits they get into, will most likely predicate how they will (or won't) communicate in response to a major disaster. "It seems that most agencies wait until something happens and then they look at interoperability," says Tony Harrison of The Public Safety Group. "The most important aspect is that if they aren't doing it on a daily basis, they're not going to do it during a disaster." The inability to properly communicate with outside personnel who are working the same incident not only hampers effective operations, but can lead to a serious breach in responder safety.

Tactical dispatchers

Another component of homeland security that was developed around the same time as the Domestic Preparedness program were Metropolitan Medical Task Forces (MMTFs), an Emergency Medical Service equivalent of the Federal Emergency Management Agency's Urban Search & Rescue task forces that are deployed to aid victims of building collapse. Many of the large cities that created MMTFs included communications as an important component of those teams.

The San Jose (Calif.) Fire Department, for example, maintains among its staff a rapid-response team of specially trained and equipped dispatchers who will deploy with a communications vehicle to establish communications, resource accountability and documentation at an incident's command post. Noting the effectiveness of this kind of team on fires and rescues, San Jose's MMTF quickly brought the Incident Dispatch Team into its response parameters.

"When the MMTF responds into the field, communication is a real key safety issue," says Edwards-Winslow. "By being able to take along incident dispatchers, we have a high level of confidence that the people who are handling our message traffic are well aware of the situation we're working in and can provide us with the highest level of cooperation and support."

Cincinnati also included communications personnel when it developed a Metropolitan Medical Response System. "Communications personnel possess the skills and forethought needed in this type of disaster," says Lisa Knapp, communications supervisor for the Cincinnati Fire Department. "They are used to multi-tasking, they are masters in the Incident Command System and radio communications, they know who and where to call for resources needed, they are consistently reviewing and creating emergency procedures for all types of disasters."

"The dispatchers bring a different perspective to the table than a first responder or an emergency manager," says Edwards-Winslow, "and it's another perspective that's really crucial in developing a full response that has safety at its core."

Dispatcher training

Perhaps the most important component of any homeland security program is the quality of training given the dispatchers responsible for it. As the preliminary link between the public and the response organization, dispatchers must be intimately familiar with department response policies and protocols, current events, current stages of alert, and related warnings that the public may be calling in about. A thorough familiarity with current events, especially as they pertain to homeland security, is vital if an agency's dispatchers are going to prevent panic and reassure its public of an agency's ability to respond to and handle terrorist activities.

"When people call and have questions or begin to describe their symptoms, dispatchers who are well-trained may pick up on clues that may be hard for someone else to recognize," says Edwards-Winslow. "If the dispatcher recognizes the symptoms, it can be a real safety factor for the first responders."

Most 911 and dispatch centers seem to be left to produce this training on their own, with limited budgets, and with limited know-how. Coordination on the statewide, if not federal, level can be a valuable component to insure appropriate and standardized training. In Oregon, for example, the state office of Emergency Management along with the Oregon Department of Public Safety Standards and Training have initiated and developed statewide targeted training for dispatch personnel specific to domestic terrorism.

Protocols and post-dispatch instructions

Some 911 centers have developed cardsets with specific questions to aid their dispatchers in asking the right kinds of questions for unusual situations, especially in the aftermath of Sept. 11, when suddenly all the paradigms changed and dispatchers realized they had to be prepared to receive calls from passengers on board hijacked aircraft or people trapped in burning high-rises.

The Palm Beach (Fla.) Communications Center developed a comprehensive flowchart protocol to handle suspicious package or exposure calls. These guidelines include key questions on identifying what makes the package suspicious, addresses caller and scene safety issues, as well as instructions for what the caller should do.

Dispatchers at the Seminole County (Fla.) Department of Public Safety got together and developed a bound cardset, modeled after the popular medical protocol systems already in place in many dispatch centers. The cards allow dispatchers to ask questions designed for specific situations such as biological agent exposure, suspicious mail, calls from aircraft. The cardset also includes important phone numbers for notification and referral.

"Interrogation aids help dispatchers tremendously," says Joe LeBlanc, senior coordinator for the Seminole County Department of Public Safety (DPS). "It will help responding agencies and it will help dispatchers to get a better understanding of the actual problem, and it generally helps the caller when the call-taker is calm and collected and has a series of questions that are asked in a logical sequence."

One way to increase homeland security and ensure the availability of immediate patient care is to provide targeted training for 911 communication center personnel. Any center equipped to receive emergency medical calls should have its call-takers trained and certified as Emergency Medical Dispatchers, specifically trained to use certified medical reference system or protocol to provide appropriate and immediate patient care advice over the phone.

"The EMD will know how to send the right thing(s), in the right way, at the right time, in the right configuration," says Robert Martin, Executive Director of the National Academies of Emergency Dispatch, certifier of dispatch protocol systems for police, fire, and EMS. "In this time of great expectations, but limited funds and severely strained resources, being able to do this effectively is paramount in establishing a solid foundation of early access to this country's emergency response system."

Networking

Perhaps the most important aspect for any agency to embrace is networking. Communication between different 911 centers is a vital component of preparations for any kind of scenario, not only homeland security. Just as different law enforcement agencies need to network to discern connections between seemingly unrelated activities, 911 dispatchers also need to be aware of warning signs detected by their neighboring agencies.

"The more that agencies at the local, state, and federal levels can network and share ideas and brainstorm on solutions, the better off we'll be in the long run," says LeBlanc. "The worst thing that can happen is to be parochial about something like that and develop something totally in the dark and not get ideas from other people in your field."

Part V

Recovery

18 Search and rescue assistance from FEMA

Ed Comeau

During the past decade, the National Urban Search and Rescue (US&R) Response System, operating under the aegis of the Federal Emergency Management Agency (FEMA), has grown to include 28 task force teams that can respond within 6 hours to any disaster site in the United States. The task force teams, complete with personnel and equipment, provide a resource local incident commanders can use at disaster scenes.

The program originally evolved in response to the need for trained personnel to assist in coping with natural disasters, primarily earthquakes. Following the Oklahoma City bombing in 1995, however, the government realized that the task forces had broader potential and began to deploy them to events, such as the 1996 Atlanta Summer Olympics, at which a catastrophic event could occur.

Personnel and equipment

Each US&R team has 62 members with at least two canines and handlers. In addition to firefighters, specialized positions on task forces can include structural engineers, communication experts, rigging specialists, and physicians specializing in trauma rescue, among others.

The equipment cache that goes with each team is standardized and comprehensive. It weighs 60,000 pounds (27,215 kilograms), costs approximately $1.4 million, and contains 16,400 pieces of equipment. It's designed to support the team for 72 hours without any outside support and includes food, water, housing, and sanitation.

The equipment cache is also made up of a specific list of rescue equipment. This list has evolved during the years based on numerous task force responses and continues to evolve. California modified its equipment list for teams that were deployed later based on the suggestions of the initial teams at Ground Zero. The equipment that is used ranges from cutting tools that can cut through reinforced concrete to telescoping cameras that can reach into small voids deep within a rubble pile.

The equipment cache is preloaded onto pallets that can be quickly loaded onto military transport planes. These loads are carefully controlled to ensure that no hazardous substances are transported, such as fuel. There are strict weight limits to ensure that the equipment and personnel can all be transported by a wide range of military aircraft, including C141s or C130s.

Deployment on September 11

As soon as news of the September 11 attacks on the World Trade Center and the Pentagon reached FEMA, the US&R task force teams were told to prepare for possible deployment.

By 7:00 a.m. Pacific Standard Time, for example, California officials had begun the process of pulling their teams together and assigning personnel.

"We were given a 'heads up' through the chain of command from OES [California Office of Emergency Services]," says Captain David Whitt of the Sacramento, California, Fire Department.

Twenty-six of the 28 US&R task forces were eventually deployed, 21 to New York City and 5 to the Pentagon. Among the five responding to the Pentagon were the Fairfax County, Virginia, and Montgomery County, Maryland, teams, based near Washington D.C. The rest of the task force teams were flown in by military aircraft from all over the country.

Normally, a task force's departure from its designated military base isn't a problem because it works closely with its respective base on departure procedures. However, all U.S. military installations were on extreme high alert, which caused some delay in processing personnel and equipment.

"We were escorted everywhere we went by a member of the National Guard and the police department," says Battalion Chief Perry Peake of the San Diego Fire and Life Safety Services and a leader of California Task Force 8. Because aircraft were at a premium, moving personnel and equipment presented an additional challenge.

"By 5:00 p.m., the task force was 'wheels up' from Travis Air Force Base," notes Whitt. Task Force 8 arrived at McGuire Air Force Base outside New York City at 3:00 a.m. Eastern Standard Time, and members were processed and boarded buses for the trip to Manhattan. By noon on September 12, they were en route to Ground Zero.

The last few miles were the longest because the area had been closed to traffic.

"It took three hours to get across the bridge to the World Trade Center," says Whitt.

On the scene at ground zero

When the task force reached the scene, its members started setting up their base of operations and began coordinating their efforts with those of the New York City Fire Department. Sadly, the job was more difficult than usual because many of the New York US&R task force had been killed. Among them was Chief Ray Downey, one of the developers of the national task force system, who'd been closely involved in the operations in Oklahoma City.

"Ray Downey was the instrumental force in the development of the Urban Search and Rescue task force system during the 1990s," says Ed Comeau, a former member of the Phoenix Arizona Fire Department US&R team who was involved in the development of the Phoenix team. "His expertise in helping not only form but train the very teams called to his rescue will be missed tremendously."

Despite the horror of the catastrophe, all those who responded spoke highly of the efforts of the New York City firefighters.

"We were treated like gold by FDNY," says Peake. "We were honored that we were able to help our fellow firefighters."

"It was a sad situation, but enormously touching. Everyone was working together under very difficult conditions," says Assistant Chief Steve Storment, of Arizona Task Force 1, from the Phoenix Fire Department.

Operational strategy

The task forces were divided into two teams, a day shift and a night shift. The teams' first assignment was to triage the area and determine the scope of the disaster, the types of buildings involved, and the best place to deploy task force personnel. After that, "the mission was straightforward," says Whitt. "Identify the void spaces, shore the void spaces, and search the void spaces."

Once the operation was established, other task forces were rotated through to provide assistance and relief. All of the US&R task forces worked under the direction of the New York City Fire Department and side by side with police officers and firefighters.

"We were split-assigned with four other task forces, and our areas were split into quadrants," explains Phoenix Fire Department Deputy Chief Russell Bovee, who was with Arizona Task Force 1, on-site from September 19 to 29. The scope of the scene was enormous, according to Bovee, who was also at the Oklahoma City bombing.

"One of the challenges was that this was the biggest rescue effort in this country. They activated all of the task forces for either the Pentagon or New York, and they were facing challenges they hadn't faced before.

"The work site was so big that it was hard to understand the complexity of it all. You could have put all of the task forces to work at the same time, and we wouldn't have seen each other," says Peake.

In all, eight task forces from California were among the 26 US&R teams deployed to the scene. This allowed the task forces that arrived later to learn from the preceding ones.

"We shared a lot of intel," says Peake. "Every day at 10:00 a.m., there'd be a conference call with all eight task forces." These calls, arranged by the California OES, continued as long as any task force from California was deployed.

"We learned a lot about what equipment to bring," notes Peake. "Those that had already deployed would report, 'We did this today, and it didn't work.' "Members of another task force on the conference call could then identify a tool that might do the job better and make sure it got to the site.

Dealing with debris

Among the unique challenges at the World Trade Center was the amount of debris that had to be moved. Most of the buildings' concrete had been pulverized, and extensive crane work was needed to get the towers' beams, some of which weighed almost a ton per running foot (0.9 metric tons per 0.3 meter), out of the way so the crews could go to work.

"We were moving away the debris not only looking for bodies or survivors," says Bovee, "but also so the cranes could work in the area. It was real time-consuming removing the beams."

"Going slower meant going faster," adds Storment, who served as safety officer for Arizona Task Force 1. "You worked more effectively because it was safer."

The enormous amounts of dust also presented health hazards.

The Environmental Protection Agency was concerned that the large amounts of burning Freon in the air conditioning systems would generate phosgene gas, reports Storment, and the smoke produced by the deep-seated fires created inhalation hazards. The fires also generated extremely high temperatures. In some areas of the debris pile, temperatures reached 1,000°F (538°C).

Conclusion

Out of the tragedies at the World Trade Center and the Pentagon on September 11 came lessons for strengthening the US&R system's ability to prepare and respond. Each task force will be assessing what worked for it. System wide lessons are also being looked at, including the need for additional funding, equipment, and training.

19 | Stress management for police officers

Rickey Hargrave

The September 11, 2001, terrorist attacks on the United States remind law enforcement executives not only of the need for prevention and response strategies but also of the tremendous impact events of this magnitude can have on rescue personnel. Chiefs of police all across America are seeking remedies to the extended trauma in their own agencies.

Helping these brave men and women find some normalization after such an extraordinary event is what chaplains attempt to do. Lessons learned by the chaplains and critical incident stress management (CISM) teams in New York can help relieve the stresses inherent in police work. This is my own story of how I responded and the lessons I learned.

After the terrorist attacks, the International Conference of Police Chaplains (ICPC) requested chaplains and CISM teams to assist the Port Authority of New York/New Jersey. The ICPC requested certified master chaplains and members of the International Critical Incident Stress Foundation (ICISF) holding advanced certification in critical incident stress management. The assignment was to contact members of the Port Authority Police Department (PAPD) in each of their 13 stations throughout the greater New York area.

One police chaplain's story

As a police chaplain with the requested qualifications, I joined in this response.

In the 16 weeks following September 11, a total of 67 ICPC chaplains responded to the PAPD, filling 108 slots. Other CISM members totaled 187. These members consisted of peer support officers from other agencies and mental health professionals trained in CISM. We were sent out in teams of three to five, depending on the vehicles available for transport. Each team had at least one chaplain.

We planned to use defusings, and, if possible, debriefings. A defusing is a three-phase, structured small group discussion provided within hours of a crisis for purposes of assessment, triaging, and acute symptom mitigation. A debriefing is a closed confidential discussion of a critical incident relating to the feelings and perceptions of those directly involved before, during, and after a stressful event. Models for group intervention, debriefings are intended to provide support, education, and an outlet for views and feelings associated with the event. Debriefings are not counseling or an operational critique of the incident.

We decided to follow as closely as possible the model of one-to-one debriefing established by Dr. Jeffery Mitchell and Dr. George Everly, professors at the University of Maryland and Loyola College, respectively (see Figure 19-1). With the extreme trauma

Figure 19-1.
The Mitchell model
of debriefing.

Critical incident stress management (CISM) is a comprehensive, integrative, multicomponent crisis intervention system. CISM is considered comprehensive because it consists of multiple crisis intervention components, which functionally span the entire temporal spectrum of a crisis. CISM interventions range from a precrisis phase through the acute crisis phase, and into the post-crisis phase. CISM is also considered comprehensive in that it consists of interventions that may be applied to individuals, small functional groups, large groups, families, organizations, and even communities.

A complete CISM would include preventative/educational/informational programs as well as the following:

- On-scene support
- Advice to command
- Demobilization services
- Formal debriefings
- Resource referral services
- Family/loved one support services
- Support to emergency management
- Support to employee assistance programs (EAP)
- Community awareness.

The Mitchell model also advances seven core components of critical incident stress management:

1. **Precrisis preparation** occurring during precrisis phase planning. It is used in anticipation of a crisis. The goals are to set expectations and improve coping stress management. The typical format is one of group organization and should include decision making staff and personnel.

2. **Demobilization and staff consult** (rescuers) involves a group information briefing for civilians, schools, and businesses. This would occur after the crisis or at the end of a shift. It is event-driven. The goals are to inform and consult with those affected by the event, allow psychological decompression, and assist in stress management. The format is that of a large group organization

3. **Defusing** occurs within 12 hours after the crisis. Defusing is usually symptom-driven, with the goals of symptom mitigation and possible closure or triage for those who may need extra help. The format is small group, possibly even one-to-one, interaction.

4. **Critical incident stress debriefing (CISD)** occurs one to seven days after the crisis. It is usually symptom-driven but can be event-driven. The goals are to facilitate psychological closure, mitigate symptoms, or perform triage. The format is small group.

5. **Individual crisis intervention** (one to one) can occur anytime, anywhere. It is symptom-driven, with the goals of symptom mitigation and a return to function, if possible. Referrals are made if needed. The format is individual and was the most often used format for us in New York.

6. **Family CISM or organization consultation** can occur at any time and is either symptom-driven or event-driven. The goals are to foster support, communications, and mitigation of symptoms; attain closure on the event, if possible; and make referrals, if needed. The format is within the organizations or family.

7. **Follow-up and referral** is a final step that can occur any time but most often after the crisis. It is usually symptom-driven. The goals are to assess mental status and access a higher level of care. The format may be either individual or family.

Adapted from George Everly and Jeffery Mitchell, *Critical Incident Stress Management (CISM): A New Era and Standard of Care in Crisis Intervention* (Ellicott City, Md.: Chevron Publishing, 1997).

event on every street and in every set of shock-widened eyes, we knew we would not be able to go into depth with these rescue personnel. Our goal was to let them know that counseling and debriefing help would be available when they needed it and to give a word of encouragement while they performed a task for which no one could prepare them....

Listening at Ground Zero

Eventually, we noticed that the rescue workers became more receptive to us. People were talking about their feelings, their hurts, thinking about family and friends they saw last week and who they hadn't seen since. Our local rescue and recovery workers were amazed by all the groups coming from all over the country to assist. New York officers and firefighters are finding they are part of a large family that includes New Jersey, Washington, Pennsylvania, Oklahoma, Texas, and parts beyond. All across this city we are experiencing a warmth and a closeness that is only evident in the most loving of families. And when families hurt, families pull together.

There was a change in the conversation. The stories at the morgue were of those who they knew had died. It was a tough duty to listen to the stories of longtime friends and all the things they used to do on and off duty. It was critical that we listen, especially with a confidential ear. The wall of confidence can be a fragile one. One breach and there may not be another opportunity to regain lost trust.

The purpose of crisis counselors in the middle of an emergency such as this is mainly one of laying a foundation and helping to address and lessen the immediate emotional and spiritual needs of the moment....

We noted the change in emotional expressiveness from one day to the other. We listened as workers spoke of the broken sleep so evident in their faces. We heard of physical problems including nausea, profuse sweating or chills, tremors, or an increased pulse rate. Some confessed to being confused and having difficulty making decisions or remembering orders or procedures. Many suffered from a sense of grief, anger, or fear of the magnitude of the event. Several expressed feelings of numbness and isolation.

The ministry of a chaplain does not predominantly involve long-term counseling. This is the reason most chaplains work well in emergency situations. On Monday, September 17, between 12:45 p.m. and 3:10 p.m., we listed 187 firefighters, police officers, medical workers, and others who visited with us personally, sometimes one on one, many times four or five on one. But always we had the same purpose: to get them to understand how much the families appreciate what they do, how much we appreciate what they do, and how much the nation appreciates what they do.

One young officer leaning on a barricade, telling folks they could not enter this area, said to me, "What good am I serving here away from the main site?" I told him that keeping these folks away from the center of the rescue effort keeps the rescuers' areas clear so they can do their work. This is a tremendous help to the effort. He wanted to do more. Of course, we all want to do more. The key is to do our job and do it well.

As I talked with this young officer about the importance of his job, my purpose became a little clearer. All the men and women with whom we talked desperately needed to know that there is stability in the chaos. We never had to bring up the subject of God or religion. It was raised for us by many of those who were talking and was phrased in their own personal belief systems. Answers were not required but understanding was. The need to express one's own belief was evident as we listened to the hearts of the officers.

Honoring the victims

Each time a transport ambulance arrived at our site we were warned whether the victim wore a uniform. If a uniform was confirmed, then every person in the area formed an honor line. When the transport arrived at its designated space, the ranks closed and snapped to attention. The call of "present arms" brought salutes from every sworn member of the police department or the fire department. Those of us who were auxiliary to this event placed our right hands over our hearts. As the gurney entered the triage station there was the call of "order arms" and we stood down. We all turned to resume our assigned duties. There is something special we were privileged to observe about the brotherhood of firefighters and police officers....

On a four-foot-by-eight-foot piece of plywood near the trailer trucks in the morgue area, we read these unsigned words:

> We are the guardians of the unknown. We see the end result of our dastardly deeds and attempt to answer questions that will reveal the true identity of these honored dead. There are no questions concerning sacrifice, courage and bravery for they have been proven by heroic actions. We play a small part in an incident that shall become an inspiration to all those who may come after.

Signs, prayers, and questions

Attention was then directed to the posters with pictures of a father or mother, a son or daughter, a husband or wife begging for information, asking, "Have you seen...?" This place seemed to invite such outpourings of emotion. Earlier that emotion had been suppressed. Now it flowed during break times. Candles, long since burned out, lined the walls leading to the office of the New York medical examiner. Each candle reminded us that people, like flames, eventually die. Flowers, some fresh, many faded, also testified to the fleeting nature of life. Officers asked about a second chance, life after death, preparation for death.

And the people came—all observed by the officers, with me beside them. Many officers would stop to read the message on the signs, many offering prayers, some just standing amid their own sweeping emotions. Some would see me and respond to my questions.

"Yes, I knew someone in the towers who died."

"I barely escaped with my life and I wondered why God would spare me?"

"We can't let terror reign, not in New York, not in America!"

"Thank you, Chaplain. I'll be alright. Just pray for those families who lost loved ones."

Teamwork on the scene

On the scene, the Disaster Mortuary Officials Response Team (D-MORT) came in to assist with the "routine" tasks of the medical examiner because death did not take a holiday after the tragedy of September 11. The state police of New York and New Jersey pulled duty shifts guarding the main entrance to the morgue. Police academy recruits directed traffic at the busy intersection of First Avenue and 30th Street. Visiting departments brought buses full of willing officers ready and able to relieve New York's finest at perimeter checkpoints. All of these groups were glad to see the chaplain rolling down the street pushing a shopping cart full of water and energy bars.

Friday, September 21, was the last day of my first tour. (I served a second tour in New York City from December 8 through 18.) Protocol planned to conduct exit interviews with all the chaplains and CISM team members. The last thing we needed was to send a lot of traumatized people back to their departments.

Debriefing the debriefer

A debriefing was scheduled for me when I returned to Texas with team members not directly affected by the incident. Debriefing of the debriefer is paramount in the process. My experience after the bombing in Oklahoma City helps explain why.

Coming home from my 10 days in Oklahoma City following the bombing of the Murrah building, things went well for about three weeks. People were talking to me and asking me about what I saw and did. I was never debriefed. Sometime in June my wife came into my study and urged me to go talk to a mental health expert. That was the first time I had any indication that I had changed. It was clear to her that I was more aloof, generally disinterested in everything. I had dropped out of my church choir and become more irritable. I called some of my chaplain friends who had some critical incident stress debriefing (CISD) skills (remember this was early in 1995) and we had a four-hour session.

That was the first time I really cried. I felt safe enough with them to express thoughts of hatred and anger as well as fear and doubt that had never been part of me before. I did not talk about these things with my wife because I would not allow her to know I was weak (this was a bad decision—she knew it already, and I had just denied it). I would not go to the pastor. I wondered how anyone who had not seen what I had could ever understand what it was like. It took all my courage to approach peers who had seen death firsthand before I started to feel normal again. Stress-related problems are real and curable if trained, concerned individuals approach them in a professional manner. Thankfully, I had some of those people around me.

Thus, I applaud the decision to have exit interviews and encourage each chaplain and team member who went to Ground Zero to have his or her own debriefing session back home....

We checked in to the command post and were told that we had to be out of town by sundown. We started driving home Friday night. No one can visit Ground Zero and remain the same. My prayer is that I will be stronger, more compassionate, and better able to assist those closest and dearest to me. I pray that I will be better able to understand the unity, hurts, fears, and discouragements of these wonderful "protectors of the gates." I hope I can help them normalize their feelings and frustrations to become better officers of the law.

Learning from the past

The emotions and feelings discussed in this selection are not reserved for major catastrophes. By learning from these major events we are better able to care for our own officers using the same principles of stress management employed in New York City. My intent was to provide law enforcement executives with a glimpse of the effectiveness of a chaplaincy and a critical incident stress management team or PEER support team.

Police departments that do not have a program like one of these in place might consider developing one. The International Conference of Police Chaplains, the International Critical Incident Stress Foundation, or numerous other organizations would be delighted to give direction in establishing an effective program. For more information on these two organizations you may consult the following web sites: http://www.icpc4cops.org or http://www.icisf.org, or you may contact the author at highview@attbi.com.

20 | Stress management for firefighters

Robert L. Smith

The events of Sept. 11, 2001, will prove to be pivotal in our nation's history. The shift in behavior and attitude that will take place in American society will have a significant impact on the attitudes and behaviors of firefighters and fire service managers.

In other words, the fire service will never be the same as it was prior to the attacks. As fire chiefs, we'll be forced to examine the way we conduct operations and how we take care of our brothers, sisters and their families. Addressing the psychological and emotional care of our firefighters has become an important aspect of our mission.

The fact that the fire service is a caretaking profession has some bearing on this discussion. Firefighters are trained and socialized to respond to the needs of others, and this mission is an important facet of the firefighter's job. Individuals in other caretaking professions, such as nurses and physicians, also are trained to respond to the needs of others. We know that job stress and burn out are issues that people in these caretaking professions should pay attention to. Consequently, we must place a higher emphasis on the psychological and emotional health of firefighters so they are physically and mentally prepared to serve the public.

New questions have developed and are being asked by fire chiefs in response to the attacks on September 11. How will we treat a high-rise fire? How will we ensure safety on the fireground during a suspected terrorist attack? Will we handle hazmat incidents differently? It's important to note that questions like these now are emotionally charged rather than simply tactical. How can we take care of our firefighters' emotional, psychological and stress management needs as these tactical questions are processed?

New approach to stress

Traditionally, fire departments have taken a response approach rather than a management approach to stress. Often, we're slow to respond until something goes wrong. We send a firefighter to addictions treatment for a drinking problem, or we mandate employee counseling sessions when behavior is problematic. As a result of this strategy, firefighters are forced to resolve their problems in a time of stress while at odds with their employer.

Instead, a management/prevention approach to stress could better serve the firefighter. The events of September 11 signaled a need to end the reactive approach. Fire service managers no longer have the luxury of waiting for a problem to occur before responding.

Figure 20-1.

Methods of stress reduction for firefighters.

1. Establish a Stress Management Unit for your organization.
2. Make contact with interested mental health practitioners and employee assistance programs that want to be involved in the stress management process of your organization. Be sure these counselors spend time in the fire stations, riding along on the apparatus and learning about how to work with fire department families based on current research.
3. Have a plan for ongoing stress education for your department. This should include stress management presentations that focus on both critical and non-critical incidents. Current research exists to support the idea that non-critical incident stress also plays a role in cumulative stress.
4. Provide basic stress education to new recruits. Firefighters are socialized or indoctrinated into their jobs. Fire chiefs and departments can supply early messages to recruits by including information about proper coping methods.
5. Provide structured mentoring for firefighters of all ranks.
6. Provide good information about stress management to your firefighters. Put information and contact numbers in the stations and provide peer contacts who are accessible to your firefighters. Police departments and industrial plants have had peer support teams for years. These individuals do not practice mental health but assist other firefighters in gathering information about stress, mental health, and mental health resources.
7. Create a way for firefighters to enter the mental health system if needed. Contract with licensed mental health practitioners in advance. The counselors and therapists who are most familiar with your department should train other therapists about your department and firefighters.
8. Listen to the new concerns of firefighters since Sept. 11. Start a continual process of assessing the newest concerns of your firefighters. How do they feel about the possibility of future attacks? Find a new way to show support for your firefighters on a regular basis, such as telling them you appreciate their efforts and visiting the stations. Address the needs of your firefighters.
9. Showcase your firefighters—get caught telling the public, the media and elected officials how good they are. Specifically, tell others about how your department is ready for disasters and further attacks.
10. Allow your firefighters to participate in addressing their job concerns. For example, create a safety committee or an advisory committee to formulate new operating guidelines or procedures. This will help your firefighters emotionally by helping them to feel in control of their job situation.

Diverse sources of stress

The management of firefighter stress is complex and multifaceted. The average firefighter encounters stress, not only from critical incidents, but also from non-critical incidents such as personality conflicts within the firehouse, family problems, common hardships of a long tour of duty or the death of a family member.

My Global Fire Service Stress Management Model strives to focus on all fire department stress rather than only on stress that is encountered by exposure to a critical incident. As stress is cumulative, it doesn't matter if the particular stressor is critical incident stress or other more routine firefighter stress.

For example, firefighters tend to be socialized as task-oriented perfectionists. Firefighters will encounter significant stress over failed equipment that hindered a rescue or a department policy that they do not agree with. In short, stress is stress—we can't overlook any of it. The Global Fire Service Stress Management Model goes beyond Critical Incident Stress Management and other models while integrating CISM as part of the package.

A department's Stress Management Unit

The Washington Township Fire Department Stress Management Unit was developed to address these critical and non-critical issues and to follow the Global Fire Service Stress Management Model. The model seeks to address difficulties early in the problem process, as early treatment is the key to effective management.

Members of the Washington Township Fire Department SMU are trained in CISM; however, the central focus of the unit is the management of multifaceted firefighter stress. The SMU is composed of one clergy member and two firefighters who are licensed as mental health practitioners to act as trainers, supervisors and facilitators.

The SMU operates in a non-intrusive manner, and the call for response is often initiated by the affected firefighters or by their supervisor. The unit's response can provide support, as well as initiate a possible assessment for further mental health assistance.

The model has several areas of concentration, including stress education, mentoring, unit response guidelines, new recruit education, spiritual care, public relations and assessment. Education includes stress awareness/management training for the firefighter as well as relationship skills workshops for spouses and families.

One example of the stress management component is the coaching of the firefighter and spouse around the single-parent phenomenon of the fire service: The spouse can be left to parent the children without assistance from the firefighter during long tours of duty and beyond, especially if a part-time job is included in that time of absence.

Unit components

Assessment is a function of the department's Stress Management Unit. All members meet for quarterly training and are introduced to basic stress management skills. The SMU in a fire department must address firefighter stress with an open-minded attitude.

However, the SMU must be a conduit to introduce firefighters into a mental health system that understands the specific needs of firefighters and their families. Too often, firefighters gain access to an unfamiliar mental health system that attempts to treat them like non-firefighters and devalues their coping mechanisms and loyalties. The SMU addresses and can improve this problem.

Pastoral care

Pastoral care is an important aspect in the model. The Washington Township Fire Department has three chaplains: a rabbi and a minister who are certified firefighters, and a Catholic priest. Members of our pastoral care staff are trained to function in both the pastoral care role and the peer counselor role. The peer training is important for pastors and mental health clinicians to become involved in and be accepted as part of the organization.

It's been shown that firefighters respond best to other firefighters as they understand the built-in coping mechanisms developed by those in the fire service. Individuals who attempt to assist firefighters should understand the nature of the occupation and the cohesion of the group. Too often, firefighters are put off by a mental health professional who fails to understand firefighter coping methods. The helper must know how to enable these socialized methods.

Internal public relations

Internal public relations is a very large consideration for the fire department SMU. Firefighters depend on the maintenance of confidentiality, loyalty and prompt service of the unit. The connection firefighters experience with members of the SMU is tantamount to the unit's success. Unit members are very aware of their image with firefighters and are selected on their merits. The unit also functions as a diplomatic arm of the fire department administration. Firefighters soon understand that the administration values their ability to function on the job without stress-related symptoms.

Unit response guidelines are an important consideration in the Global Fire Service Stress Management Model. The SMU has responded to conflicts in fire stations, in addition to being called on to assist hospitalized firefighters or firefighters on light duty. At times, SMU members provide a meal or transportation to another firefighter in need. These examples range from simple acts of kindness to the referral for more complicated mental health intervention. The goal of all responses is to enable proper coping and assist the firefighter in the reduction of stress.

New recruit education

New recruit education and firefighter mentoring are additional aspects of the Global Fire Service Stress Management Model. New recruits at the Washington Township Fire Department receive training in stress management and coping techniques as a part of their fire academy curriculum.

Each new recruit is assigned a mentor from the SMU. The mentors assist with orienting new recruits to their assignments in a manner that promotes development of appropriate coping techniques and good mental health awareness. In addition, they teach many of the emotional mechanics of the fire service job. These include getting along with other firefighters in the new environment and the introduction of spouses and family members to the fire service circle.

Stress as a cumulative phenomenon

Many interventions exist to assist firefighters in this time of stress. The fire service must begin to recognize stress as a cumulative phenomena. Firefighters should learn in advance how to deal with the stress from critical incidents such as the ones in New York, Washington and Pennsylvania on September 11, 2001. Firefighters who respond to critical incidents in a lower state of stress have a greater chance of sustaining psychological wellness and avoiding burnout during their career.

Critical incident debriefing

A fire department plan for critical incident stress debriefing is essential. This should encompass two areas: lower-profile incidents and large-scale critical incidents.

Unfortunately, many departments don't have a plan for handling these types of large-scale incidents. Departments shouldn't depend on outside agencies alone to formulate this plan. A department representative should be involved in the planning stages because fire department managers know their personnel best.

A fire department's plan for a large incident should include the following:

- The lead mental health practitioner should be familiar with the firefighters of your department, their job roles and your organization.

- The counselor or therapist should have exposure to the fire station environment and should build rapport with the firefighters in your department.

- The lead counselor should have a license to practice mental health and should have access to the latest research about the mental health care of firefighters.

- The involvement of a qualified CISM team is essential. The team should be fully trained, experienced and include other firefighters.

- Firefighters are most comfortable talking to other firefighters. While others may be well intentioned, they may not have the same credibility as a CISM team composed of firefighters trained in Critical Incident Stress Management.

- Department chaplains should be involved in the response to a large-scale incident. Fire chiefs should commission chaplains of firefighter-represented denominations prior to a tragedy.

- Fire departments should have stress-related material available for both critical incidents and stress prevention. Departments should consider seminars and classes that address stressors other than critical incidents prior to a tragedy. Tragedies can be easier to handle if fire departments adopt a stance of prevention.

- Protocols should be developed to direct fire departments to assist families in the event of line-of-duty death or injury. Family care should be considered when long deployments of firefighters are necessary. Families could need extra assistance due to the combination effect of an absent spouse and the emotional hardships of worrying about their firefighter family member.

Your department can make a difference. We'll have better prepared and more effective rescuers if we work to reduce stress before large incidents.

21 | Line-of-duty deaths: What to do

Chris DeChant

Most fire departments never will experience firefighter fatalities on the same scale that the New York Fire Department did following the terrorist attack on the World Trade Center. Nonetheless, death is an inherent risk surrounding any local, state or federal public safety organization.

The U.S. armed forces are well aware of this reality and have a long history of providing line-of-duty death benefits ranging from legal advice to life insurance benefits for surviving family members. In contrast, many fire departments throughout the United States currently don't have any management system for firefighter deaths and won't be prepared when one occurs.

Line-of-duty death facts

Firefighters risk their lives to protect the public. It isn't a question of whether a firefighter may be killed in the line of duty. The question is how many and when. Of course, fire departments are often caught off-guard by the death of one of their own and may be ill-prepared to deal with the emotional issues surrounding such a personal trauma. Although a fire agency should help handle the difficulties encountered by the survivors, this task can become overwhelming when performed alongside an investigation and other necessary tragedy-prompted tasks.

A line-of-duty death (LODD) involves many different aspects of urgent responsibility. In addition to an investigation, the most important task becomes handling the needs of a grief-stricken family. The potential to neglect a family's needs would be the greatest injustice that a fire department could perpetrate. The family will remember not only the devastating tragedy of the death, but also all of the events, both positive and negative, following the catastrophe.

How prepared is your fire department to handle an LODD? In 1999 I completed a study involving 18 Arizona fire departments with memberships of 17 to 1,103 firefighters each. They served populations from 3,800 to 405,000 and responded to between 2,300 and 71,000 calls per year. The study also included five departments from throughout the country that had experienced an LODD. These ranged from 28 to 1,200 sworn personnel who served populations from 4,500 to 1.2 million and responded to between 60 and 120,000 calls per year. Both populations included fire chiefs and firefighters, and the LODD department studies also included surviving family members.

Comparative methodology was used to evaluate fire department LODD preparedness from the perspectives of those who had been or may be affected by an LODD. The results found that 61% of Arizona fire departments and 50% of those that had experienced a firefighter death did not have any line-of-duty death policy or procedure implemented. Clearly, more departments need to prepare for the devastating possibility of such an event.

Originally published as "Protocol for the Fallen," this article originally appeared in the December 2001 issue of *Fire Chief* magazine and is republished here with permission of PRIMEDIA Business Magazines & Media Inc. Copyright 2001, PRIMEDIA Business Magazines & Media Inc. All rights reserved.

Strategic plan development

A strategic plan should be in place when addressing an LODD. A fire department can become overwhelmed by the immediate needs surrounding the crisis and lose track of all objectives that need to be accomplished. If this happens, the operational needs may prevent a strategic and organizational approach from being developed.

The management of an LODD should be conducted with the same thoroughness and professionalism with which the department combats fire. A death requires myriad tasks and objectives which may take days, weeks or months to accomplish, necessitating that it be approached in a systematic manner, much like a complicated campaign fire.

For this reason, a fire department should implement a command system to allow increased span of control. An effective system is designed to provide a thorough systematic approach that is easy to recognize and follow. For example, The Phoenix Regional Standard Operating Procedure 201.01 states:

> Command procedures are designed to: Fix the responsibility for command on a certain individual through a standard identification system.... Ensure that a strong command will be established from the onset of the incident.... Establish an effective incident organization defining the incident commander's responsibilities.... Provide a system to process information to support incident management, planning, and decision making.

The fireground command system can be applied in the same manner with line-of-duty deaths to ensure that operations do not fail in the areas of:

- Action
- Planning
- Command and control
- Coordination
- Organization
- Safety
- Communications.

The fireground command system can be applied best for conducting an LODD event through the development and use of standard operating procedures and written representations of a department's philosophy or strategy.

The FALLEN FF incident command system

A fire department can apply the command model for responding to families of fallen firefighters as a way to develop and revamp its procedures as needed. The model explains the necessary functions and applications of a standard operating procedure. It can be divided into five main areas:

- Establishment of a standard procedure
- Training
- Application
- Review and critique
- Revision.

If a fire department implements this model, it will gain a structured plan that can be applied, reviewed and revised as necessary.

Fire departments should construct and implement an LODD standard operating procedure and then use the model to further develop, evaluate and revise the procedure as necessary. An infrastructure also must be developed for coordination of all necessary tasks. Departments can use the LODD action plan—Logistics, Empathy, and Nurturing for Fire Department Families (FALLEN FF)—as an infrastructure to organize their department in such a way.

Critical incident stress management (CISM)   CISM surrounding an LODD may be neither quick nor easy for a department to deal with. Continued support for firefighters and families may last as long as a year or longer. Although CISM is a structured mechanism for the department to assist the firefighters and family, it can begin at a more basic level through the use of advocacy, which can provide an adjunct to family and friends unwilling or unable to participate with CISM.

Investigation   An investigation of an LODD is a painful but necessary function that must be conducted to ensure that the same situation doesn't happen in the future. The investigation involves many different objectives, requiring the branch to be multifaceted and adaptive as the situation requires.

Funeral   The funeral branch can be the most important branch concerning the family, fire personnel and the public, because it affords a time and place to remember the victim and face the loss. This branch must be in place prior to an incident to provide an honorable service for the victim.

Notification   This branch will attempt to make contact with the family in a caring manner while also being honest and direct. Several main principles must be followed: notification in person, in time and with certainty; in pairs; in plain language; and with compassion.

Public information   Line-of-duty deaths generate widespread media coverage locally as well as nationally. Proper relationships with the media should help to prevent negative results that can occur when the media are inaccurately briefed or not briefed at all. This branch should be initiated at multiple stages, including: at the scene, the hospital, the funeral, the family's home and for an after-action report.

Hospital   This branch will coordinate with hospital officials for the allocation of waiting areas for family, co-workers, and the media. Another function is securing a firefighter as a hospital liaison between the medical staff and the family.

Financial   An individual should be designated to handle monetary donations to the family and ensure proper accountability for the funds.

Family liaison   This branch will provide general support for the family, including screening calls and visits, providing transportation, and assisting in coordination with other branches and their functions.

It's recommended that this system and infrastructure use a cooperative effort of labor and management to accomplish the intended goals. The importance of labor-management cooperation is an integral part of the success of this system. The cooperative effort will pair an International Association of Fire Fighters (IAFF) union member with each chief officer assigned as branch commander. This design will facilitate accomplishment of tasks and avoid duplication of effort, while also providing a secondary plan to ensure that at least one qualified person will be present to manage each branch. The IAFF is an invaluable source of LODD investigation protocol.

An integral aspect of fire department preparation and an initial stage of implementation is the completion of an emergency notification information data sheet by each employee. A sample can be found in the National Fallen Firefighters Foundation Taking Care of Our Own instruction manual. [To view or download the latest version of this form, go to www.firehero.org under the Fire Programs-Training section. You may also order a copy of the Resource Guide online or by calling 301-447-1365.]

Coordinating the response

After implementing a standard operating procedure and the FALLEN FF command system, a department must gather the necessary resources to conduct all tasks involved with a LODD. They include:

Local resources, such as

- Mortuaries and cemeteries
- Police
- Local benefits
- Medical examiner
- Media.

State resources, such as

- State benefits
- The Department of Transportation.

National resources, such as

- The National Fallen Firefighters Foundation
- The Federal Bureau of Investigation and the Bureau of Alcohol, Tobacco, and Firearms
- The National Transportation Safety Board
- Federal benefits
- Public Safety Officers Benefits Program
- National Institute for Occupational Safety and Health
- U.S. Fire Administration
- National Fire Protection Agency
- Equipment manufacturers
- The International Association of Firefighters and the International Association of Fire Chiefs.

The fire department also must have a designated system to activate the FALLEN FF command system once an event occurs. The suggested method would be through the dispatch agency with a text-messaging pager system that could alert all infrastructure members at any time. If a department were to use such a system, the on-duty commander could alert the dispatch center after a line-of-duty event occurs, resulting in activation of the infrastructure and assembly of the FALLEN FF branch officers.

After activation, the incident commander of the FALLEN FF system would receive all necessary information and reports to ensure that all tasks were being completed in a timely manner. The incident commander would then be able to acknowledge completed tasks through the use of tactical worksheets.

The incident commander should be the operations chief of the fire department to facilitate operation of the system unless this same chief was the incident commander of the event involving the death. Although the recommendations are for branch officers to be fire department chief officers, the FALLEN FF system should be utilized using any rank of fire department member. This incident command structure is similar to any other command structure and can be expanded or reduced as necessary for the department or event.

Other aspects

A fire department member also must become familiar with the benefits surrounding local, state and federal governments to assist the family during its time of need. The fire department member assigned this task will assist with benefit coordination under the financial branch officer. This function will be a great asset to ensure that all awarded benefits are distributed to the family not only during the time surrounding the event, but in the future as well. The support will allow the family to concentrate on grieving rather than on financial concerns.

A fire department also should be prepared to provide funeral services for its members. The most effective way to accomplish this goal is through the development of a fire department honor guard. The events surrounding a LODD will not be forgotten by those that it affects, and some events may be developed into traditions and memorials to those that have passed. If a fire department is unsure of how to develop and maintain an honor guard, the National Fallen Firefighters Foundation in Emmitsburg can provide information.

I cannot emphasize enough the importance of developing and instituting a LODD standard operating procedure. Due to fire service culture, fire department members have blind faith in their leaders when unsure of their department's preparedness. The FALLEN FF incident command system should be the beginning of fire department preparedness that must continue to evolve and progress for successful internal customer service.

Although this system provides a "hard" customer service format for fire departments to follow, the "soft" aspect of this system will become the difficult process to implement. Affected families only will be concerned with the end product, not the labor by which it was achieved. It's recommended that fire chiefs and their organizations become better prepared for line-of-duty deaths to ensure that they don't fail their department family members when it counts the most.

Part VI

Conclusion

22 The local role in fighting terrorism

Philip M. McVey

A whole is only as strong as its individual parts. This truism applies to everything from physical structures to social institutions. It should also apply to U.S. law enforcement as these dedicated professionals prepare to defend the nation against acts of terrorism.

Since September 11, 2001, many local law enforcement professionals have become somewhat apprehensive about projecting a positive response to the threat of terrorism. Most are anxiously looking to the federal government for direction and the all-important funding of new units and other activities that may become necessary in the national defense effort.

Dilemma facing law enforcement professionals

Due to the federal government's overwhelming financial and intelligence-gathering resources, it is only reasonable in most instances for local law enforcement agencies to defer to federal authorities in this manner. In addition, since terrorism has not generally fallen within the operational realm of local law enforcement, many agencies are concerned that they may act in a way that is counterproductive to future strategic policies.

This describes the current dilemma for many local law enforcement professionals. They can do nothing and wait for direction, or they can do something that may possibly be wrong. Unfortunately, history clearly demonstrates that when a nation becomes engaged in a war against a guerrilla organization operating in its terrorist phase, waiting can put local law enforcement so far behind the resulting operational curve that it may not recover without incurring significant capital resource losses.

Fortunately, there is a third alternative for local law enforcement. It begins with the basic realization that any proposal forthcoming from federal agencies will likely be only strategically general. Thus, each jurisdiction will have to interpret such a proposal according to the area's unique risk factors and operational capabilities. Given this, each agency must lay the necessary groundwork in preparation for these proposals by generating and incorporating into its individual administrative paradigm a basic understanding of the terrorist risks it faces and its own incident management capability.

In other words, everyone in local law enforcement needs to be able to exhibit the same operational competency level when counterterrorist campaigns are begun in their jurisdictions. This will enhance the effectiveness and efficiency of future efforts at managing the risks inherent in such endeavors. Initially, even this rudimentary task may seem a daunting effort. But it requires only three basic steps that can be implemented with a minor outlay of resources.

Originally published as "An Effective Homeland Defense Partnership." Reprinted from *The Police Chief*, Vol. LXIX, No. 4, pages 174–180, April, 2002. Copyright held by the International Association of Chiefs of Police, 515 North Washington Street, Alexandria, VA 22314 USA. Further reproduction without express written permission from IACP is strictly prohibited.

Step 1: Toward a common definition of terrorism

First, it is crucial that a common definition of terrorism be developed within and between agencies. Unfortunately, a good definition of terrorism is hard to find, principally because most definitions tend to be only partially applicable to the types of situations local law enforcement may encounter. In addition, some definitions focus on a macro law enforcement level of international or national government policy and are not germane to local law enforcement activity.

The definition, therefore, must be universally valid and must reliably serve the interests of local law enforcement jurisdictions by being both flexible and relevant. It also must be easily understood and capable of setting parameters within which the agency's risk assessments and management proposals can be designed and implemented.

A comparison of traditional criminal behavior and terrorism

Consistent with that goal, it is important to draw a parallel between traditional law enforcement criminal activities and guerrilla-inspired terrorism. Terrorism, such as we see today, is a type of politicized criminal conduct. Thus, within the occupational parameters of local law enforcement, it is much like any other criminal behavior and can best be defined by its unique attributes.

Generally, the type of terrorism that local agencies may encounter emerges from the phenomenon of contemporary guerrilla warfare. This type of warfare differs radically from guerrilla warfare of the past and is unique to the social milieu of the 20th and 21st centuries.

Contemporary guerrilla groups usually evolve just like other social groups. During a transition from individual activist to terrorist-guerrilla warrior, the person becomes more hardened and his or her ideology is radicalized. This requires a fundamental transformation of the terrorist's social organization.

Terrorist acts can be identified as being criminal in nature, symbolically targeted, and always aggressive. Terrorists seek to achieve political goals and communicate a message. Crimes manifesting these elements should be considered as the focus of any risk assessments and management policies.

Elements of terrorism

A brief discussion of these elements helps explain the phenomenon and provide the law enforcement executive with a more reliable paradigm for operational planning:

Terrorism is criminal in nature. Virtually all terrorist acts violate some criminal statutes of the host jurisdiction. This is usually the easiest element for local law enforcement to appreciate.

The targets are typically symbolic. This is a typical distinction between terrorism and guerrilla warfare where the targets are instrumental to a successful military operation. Specifically, the attacks on the World Trade Center and the Pentagon were symbolic acts designed to demonstrate to like-minded people that America was vulnerable and that it was time to rise up and follow the hijackers' lead in defeating the "Great Satan."

The actions of the terrorist serve a two-fold communicative purpose in their symbolism. In the case of the September 11, 2001, attacks, the message to Americans was that they should fear a future controlled by these terrorists. To sympathizers, the message was that they should exclusively venerate the activists' courage and deeds because the terrorists alone have sufficient strength to oppose the West.

Terrorists' actions are always aggressive and often violent. Both the threat of these acts and the use of violence are calculated to maximize the communicative and disruptive effects of the attacks.

Terrorists' goals are political. Regardless of the purported philosophy of terrorists, their ultimate goal is always enhanced political power. This is for the purpose of either taking control of the host government through illegitimate means or of influencing the government in a way that the terrorist organization's goals are eventually achieved "legitimately."

The terrorists' purpose is to communicate. Terrorism is the guerrilla warrior's ad campaign. All the points of the terrorist group's official communiqué to the faithful are embedded in its words and actions. In the terror phase of their campaign, terrorists are advocating either joining or assisting the movement in its efforts to change the political landscape. The message to the victims and their protectors is to stay out of the way or more terror will be forthcoming.

This definitional framework is practically relevant for law enforcement executives. By employing this definition, the local law enforcement agency cannot only properly label actual events occurring in its jurisdiction, but it can also provide itself with an operational matrix from which the next two steps can be achieved.

Step 2: Risk assessment

...[E]ach law enforcement agency must assess its own unique risk potential as a terrorist genesis site (creation site), a host (where it thrives), a campaign site (where a part or all of the attack would be carried out), or merely a planning base for operations in adjacent jurisdictions. Each of these possibilities carries its own risk factors.

When assessing a jurisdiction's overall risk level, it is essential that law enforcement executives avoid a type of myopia that may focus on one particular form of terrorism to the exclusion of others. Law enforcement's current effort is a war against terrorism as a whole. If these leaders become too focused on international or transnational terrorist groups, and exclude domestically generated groups, the results could be disastrous. Therefore, police chiefs must also include domestic groups espousing terrorism as a means of obtaining political goals involving, for example, animal rights, environmental protection, or ethnic identity.

Fortunately, risk assessments are easy to complete and require few resources. In fact, most law enforcement professionals conduct them every day on both the departmental and individual levels. On the department level, administrators routinely place patrol units in certain areas to cover risks associated with identified crime patterns. A risk assessment is merely probability theory applied to tangible conditions.

Probability theory in action

Both sides in a terrorist campaign typically attempt to employ probability theory to achieve and maintain an advantage. The terrorist tries to find the softest target to get the most results while expending the fewest resources. The law enforcement agency must assess the risk to particular targets within its jurisdiction and attempt to harden the ones most likely to be struck. This exercise is conducted so the terrorist will see the decreased probability for success and be deterred from acting. The secret in this type of dynamic probability analysis is to stay one or two steps ahead of the terrorist campaign.

Probability theory holds that certain axiomatic circumstances arise from the inclusion or exclusion of certain relevant variables. These are typically referred to as if-then relationships. For example, if something is present or missing from a situation, then how will its presence or absence influence the outcome?

The four parts of risk assessment

The particular procedure necessary for such an analysis of local law enforcement jurisdictions can be readily accomplished by dividing the risk assessment process into four individual arts: (1) external general, (2) external specific, (3) internal general, and (4) internal specific. Each individual part has a weighted probability that corresponds to the actual risk inherent in the jurisdiction. The first three categories generally measure the acquired risk; the last measures the institutional ability to minimize that same risk. Overall, the risk ascribed by this analysis is weighted not only by the terrorist's operational abilities but also by those of the local agency. The categories are as follows:

External general   The first variables are of a general nature that is not related to any specific circumstances within the jurisdiction. They refer to external factors that can create a climate conducive for contemporary guerrilla activity in the world and may lead (if other variables are present) to the injection of the activity into a local jurisdiction if relevant targets exist. The factors are as follows:

Geopolitical: Are political events occurring in the world that may provide recruits for any guerrilla group or for foreign support of any local activist groups?

Economic: Have financial problems arisen that may cause disruptions in a nation whose ethnic/religious demographic groups are present in the local police agency's jurisdiction?

Ideological: Have any new ideas arisen in universities or other social settings that may be cause for concern and potentially target individuals, corporations, or government entities in the area?

Guerrilla: Are guerrilla groups forming in the world that can operate in the local police agency's jurisdiction? Have nuclear, biological, or chemical weapons been threatened or deployed in the terrorist phase of any group?

Historical examples of local effects from outside activities include Ruby Ridge and Oklahoma City; the Persian Gulf War in the early 1990s and both World Trade Center attacks; and governmental environmental policies and the Unabomber's actions, to name just a few.

The preceding factors present issues of a national or international concern with potentially serious local law enforcement ramifications. If any of the above variables are present, then the local jurisdiction should begin a closer look at the next set of external variables.

External specific   These are events in the world that have a specific relationship to the jurisdiction in question. These variables focus on questions regarding the general environment and its conduciveness to immediate guerrilla group formation and operations.

Weather: Is the current weather conducive to supporting a campaign of terrorism likely to hinder a counter-terrorist operation?

Population demographics: Is there a population conducive to the guerrilla's campaign message within the jurisdiction or in any of its surrounding environs? Is the population capable of unhindered infiltration by the group?

Target access viability: Are roads and airfields available and rivers navigable? Approach and withdrawal are not always made by land. These issues are important to the terrorist group, since it is normally small and must conserve its numbers.

If the preceding external variables are present, then the environmental groundwork has been laid for the possible creation of guerrilla events with geography conducive to begin to either form or operate in the local jurisdiction.

Internal general   These are the events within a jurisdiction that have a general relationship to the formation of terrorist groups within the area.

Increased activism: Has there been any increase in indigenous radical group activity in either group formation (this includes formation of local chapters of national organizations), literature distribution, or guest speakers in target populations?

New local organizations: Have new organizations been founded that espouse radical or violent solutions to political issues? Have new spokespersons appeared locally to promote those causes?

Initiating violence: Have there been any acts of political violence, threats against government officials, or an increase in the amount of well-planned robberies that take larger than normal amounts of cash?

Increased ordnance: Have police seized large arms caches, or have there been unusual thefts of weapons from sporting goods stores, armories, or explosives from construction sites.

Politically motivated intelligence gathering: Has there been surveillance by these groups of police or government offices, corporate locations, or recognized symbolic targets within the jurisdiction?

If any or all of the preceding factors are present in a jurisdiction, then the area is experiencing the growth, formation, and activity of an activist group that may easily and quickly turn into a guerrilla organization that will soon manifest a terrorist phase.

If it is an international group that is coming into the area, this limited evaluation should suffice. The local arm terrorist organization would likely be underdeveloped.

If the group is indigenous to the jurisdiction, there will be signs of the movement and the individuals that constitute it in the local area. If that is the case, local law enforcement must immediately begin to preempt the further evolution of the guerrilla campaign. The ability to do so is the focus of the last set of risk assessment variables.

Internal specific   These are the variables that represent the counter-terrorist ability specific to the jurisdiction's resources.

Expertise: What is the level of training in the areas necessary for the creation of an effective crisis management operation? A survey of all personnel regarding their relevant knowledge must be conducted.

Training: Is there a sufficient level of training available to effectively operate a counter-terrorism unit during the campaign? The dedication of certain members to a rigorous training schedule to increase expertise in areas of deficiency should start immediately.

Preparation: Has a crisis management organization been established and practice drills accomplished to ensure its operational efficiency?

Liaison: Have liaisons been established with all the internal and adjacent jurisdictions along with civilian groups and target security operations?

Law enforcement executives should always recognize that any risk assessment must be as eclectic and dynamic as is the targeted phenomena. That applies to the following risk management procedures as well. This is a game of chess played without the other side seeing the opponent's pieces. Therefore, each move and counter-move must be anticipated to such a degree that the guerrilla organization will find the target jurisdiction so hard to attack that it will go elsewhere.

The impact of the final set of variables has a direct correlation to the weight of those preceding. The impact of a properly prepared law enforcement agency should not be underestimated. One that exhibits such a presence can easily deflect a terrorist group's intentions onto a surrounding jurisdiction that has not become as well prepared and thereby offers a much softer targeting environment. Therefore, the next step in this process provides a vehicle by which the final set of variables can be implemented.

Step 3: The response plan

The third step to exhibiting operational competency in meeting a terrorist incident is the devising of a plan to minimize or negate the threat. This must occur immediately upon the completion of the risk assessment and before any local insurgent activity.

On the strategic level, a crisis management organization (CMO) should be formed to implement the department's planning. This organization should consist of a crisis response team (CRT) as the overarching tactical unit, and various specialized subunits. Within each subunit should be included elements emphasizing its specific predetermined functions along with the necessary elements of command, control, and communication.

This is the initial phase in jurisdictional target hardening, and it becomes an integral factor in the overall deterrence equation that a guerrilla group will consider when targeting a host area.

The CMO's overall strategic responsibilities will consist of supplying local jurisdictions within its organizational parameters with a centralized redoubt in the event of an attack and will include both the CRT and its subunits until their emergence is required.

Subunits of the Critical Response Team

The CRT is the tactical unit responsible for manifesting the strategic operational plan of the CMO. Therefore, to accomplish that goal it should include the following subunits with its corresponding interrelated duties and responsibilities.

Law enforcement liaison unit   This is a proactive subunit responsible for maintaining cooperation and continued integration of all related functions between the law enforcement members and/or agencies involved in the crisis response team.

Emergency operations center   This is a reactive subunit that operates as the headquarters function of the CRT throughout the counterguerrilla campaign and subsequent follow-up operations.

Intelligence unit   This is a proactive subunit that is the most important element of the functioning operation. Its primary functions include the gathering of information for the team and the creation of a relevant database regarding the situation while assisting in making predictions regarding the guerrilla operations and advising the operational headquarters of possible countering actions. This need not be a CIA-size unit. It merely requires the local agencies to intimately know their individual jurisdictions.

Logistics unit   This is a reactive subunit charged with maintaining all the material resources of the CRT and CMO.

Operations unit   This is a reactive subunit that is responsible for the daily operations of the CRT, its individual subunits, and other possible counterguerrilla operatives embedded in those units (such as SWAT, arson-explosives, and hostage negotiators).

Civilians unit   This is a proactive liaison subunit between law enforcement and the necessary civilian components of the system. This subunit adds additional intelligence resources (such as neighborhood watch groups, sheriff's posses, and local cattleman's associations) and also allows for the incorporation of private security operatives working for the highest risk targets to integrate themselves into the CRT.

Media liaison unit   This is a reactive subunit responsible for countering the guerrilla's propaganda campaign and insuring good media relations.

Legal unit   This is a reactive subunit responsible for countering the guerrilla's attorneys (and they will come forward to use the legal system against the jurisdiction). The CRT's attorneys must be security checked since they will have access to the information of the organization.

Core mission

Each subunit must be prepared to work independently (in case it becomes isolated after a terrorist incident) and also as part of the whole. If a department lacks the resources to implement such an organization, a countywide or regional approach should be considered. At a minimum, even a two-person department should be able to act as a subunit to implement its jurisdictional intelligence function and contribute to the CRT's overall information collection capabilities.

Conclusion

The type of organizational format presented here should be flexible and general enough to be adaptable to any local agency requirements. If implemented, this creative effort will virtually guarantee a smooth transition into a counterterrorist operation and enhance a jurisdiction's probability for success by reducing the assessed risk and minimizing the damage.

Remember that terrorist acts almost always occur in local law enforcement jurisdictions. The first responders on the scene will be local law enforcement and fire personnel. The measures and planning taken before that next event will heavily influence the outcome of the overall campaign for both the target jurisdiction and the nation as a whole.

In this struggle, the efforts of local law enforcement are an integral part of the overall national defense network It will demand planning, cooperation, and dedication to the ultimate goal of winning the war. Only when all the participants in the nation's domestic defense are on the same readiness level and prepared for the fight to come can they hope to make a meaningful contribution. The probability of success in these efforts will be directly related to the hard work expended by both sides.

23 | The U.S. Homeland Security Advisory System

Thomas Ridge

The Homeland Security Advisory System will provide a comprehensive and effective means to disseminate information regarding the risk of terrorist attacks to Federal, State, and local authorities and to the American people.

As part of a series of initiatives to improve coordination and communication among all levels of government and the American public in the fight against terrorism, President Bush signed Homeland Security Presidential Directive 3, creating the Homeland Security Advisory System (HSAS). The advisory system will be the foundation for building a comprehensive and effective communications structure for the dissemination of information regarding the risk of terrorist attacks to all levels of government and the American people.

The Attorney General will be responsible for developing, implementing and managing the system. In conjunction with the development of this new system, the Attorney General will open a 45-day comment period in order to seek the views of officials at all levels of government, law enforcement and the American public. Ninety days after the conclusion of the comment period, the Attorney General in coordination with the Director of the Office of Homeland Security—will present a final Homeland Security Advisory System to the President for approval. The Homeland Security Advisory System will provide the following:

National framework

There are many federal alert systems in our country—each tailored and unique to different sectors of our society: transportation, defense, agriculture, and weather, for example. These alert systems fill vital and specific requirements for a variety of situations in both the commercial and government sectors. The Homeland Security Advisory System will provide a national framework for these systems, allowing government officials and citizens to communicate the nature and degree of terrorist threats. This advisory system characterizes appropriate levels of vigilance, preparedness and readiness in a series of graduated Threat Conditions. The Protective Measures that correspond to each Threat Condition will help the government and citizens decide what action they take to help counter and respond to terrorist activity. Based on the threat level, Federal agencies will implement appropriate Protective Measures. States and localities will be encouraged to adopt compatible systems.

Factors for assignment of Threat Conditions

The Homeland Security Advisory System will provide a framework for the Attorney General, in consultation with the Director of the Office of Homeland Security, to assign

Originally published as *Governor Ridge Announces Homeland Security Advisory System,* Office of Homeland Security, Executive Office of the President, White House, Washington, D.C., March 12, 2002. On January 24, 2003, Governor Ridge was sworn in as Secretary of Homeland Security.

Threat Conditions, which can apply nationally, regionally, by sector or to a potential target. Cabinet Secretaries and other members of the Homeland Security Council will be consulted as appropriate. A variety of factors may be used to assess the threat. Among these:

- Is the threat credible?
- Is the threat corroborated?
- Is the threat specific and/or imminent?
- How grave is the threat?

Unified system for public announcements

Public announcements of threat advisories and alerts help deter terrorist activity, notify law enforcement and State and local government officials of threats, inform the public about government preparations, and provide them with the information necessary to respond to the threat. State and local officials will be informed in advance of national threat advisories when possible. The Attorney General will develop a system for conveying relevant information to Federal, State, and local officials, and the private sector expeditiously. Heightened Threat Conditions can be declared for the entire nation, or for a specific geographic area, functional or industrial sector. Changes in assigned Threat Conditions will be made when necessary.

A tool to combat terrorism

Threat Conditions characterize the risk of terrorist attack. Protective Measures are the steps that will be taken by government and the private sector to reduce vulnerabilities. The HSAS establishes five Threat Conditions with associated suggested Protective Measures:

Low condition: Green

Low risk of terrorist attacks. The following Protective Measures may be applied:

- Refining and exercising preplanned Protective Measures
- Ensuring personnel receive training on HSAS, departmental, or agency-specific Protective Measures
- Regularly assessing facilities for vulnerabilities and taking measures to reduce them.

Guarded condition: Blue

General risk of terrorist attack. In addition to the previously outlined Protective Measures, the following may be applied:

- Checking communications with designated emergency response or command locations
- Reviewing and updating emergency response procedures
- Providing the public with necessary information.

Elevated condition: Yellow

Significant risk of terrorist attacks. In addition to the previously outlined Protective Measures, the following may be applied:

- Increasing surveillance of critical locations
- Coordinating emergency plans with nearby jurisdictions

- Assessing further refinement of Protective Measures within the context of the current threat information
- Implementing, as appropriate, contingency and emergency response plans.

High condition: Orange

High risk of terrorist attacks. In addition to the previously outlined Protective Measures, the following may be applied:

- Coordinating necessary security efforts with armed forces or law enforcement agencies
- Taking additional precaution at public events
- Preparing to work at an alternate site or with a dispersed workforce
- Restricting access to essential personnel only.

Severe condition: Red

Severe risk of terrorist attacks. In addition to the previously outlined Protective Measures, the following may be applied:

- Assigning emergency response personnel and pre-positioning specially trained teams
- Monitoring, redirecting or constraining transportation systems
- Closing public and government facilities
- Increasing or redirecting personnel to address critical emergency needs.

24

The future of homeland security

Roger L. Kemp

Federal and state elected leaders and administrators have made substantial progress in the field of homeland security since September 2001. City and county managers and their elected officials, however, are at the forefront of this movement. After all, local government employees were the first responders to the terrorist acts of September 11. While national and state leadership is essential, the future of homeland security depends on the implementation of preparedness initiatives at the local level. Local appointed and elected leaders have developed new emergency management practices and techniques, have applied new computer software to this field, and have begun to modify municipal and county codes to initiate as well as enhance safeguards to protect their citizens. All of these new measures fall into one or more of the four phases of emergency management: mitigation, preparedness, response, and recovery.

In less than two years, states have standardized many practices in emergency management for cities and counties within their respective boundaries. The national government has responded with a new federal department, the Department of Homeland Security, created in January 2003. As the department takes shape, coordination among federal agencies in the area of homeland security should improve. Equally important, federal departments are initiating training programs to educate city and county officials in emergency management. Many of these state-of-the-art practices and trends have been examined in this volume.

Figure 1-2 showed that of the best practices examined in this volume, twenty-one address the preparedness phase, seventeen come under the response phase, fifteen fall under the mitigation phase, and eleven come under the recovery phase. This may suggest that the priorities for development of additional best practices are response, mitigation, and recovery.

A number of new practices are evolving, and the remainder of this selection summarizes the most important of these evolving practices, as well as major trends in the new field of homeland security. They are categorized by the different phases of emergency management in Figure 24-1. City and county managers throughout the nation should pay special attention to the evolving best practices in this field, since the public not only expects, but demands, that local officials take the necessary steps to safeguard their life and property during times of disaster, whether natural or man-made.

Mitigation

Federal assistance programs Selection 3 presented the numerous federal programs available to assist local officials in the mitigation phase of their emergency management plans. It noted the specialized training programs provided by the Federal Emergency Management Agency, the U.S. Fire Administration, the Federal Bureau of Investigation, and the Departments of Justice, Health and Human Services, Defense, and Energy. Contacts should be made directly with these organizations to determine the details,

Figure 24-1.

Best practices and trends in homeland security by phases of emergency management.

Mitigation

Federal assistance programs
U.S. Homeland Security Advisory System
Threat assessment
Building design and physical structures
Municipal and county building codes
Nonstructural safety measures
Pedestrian and vehicular evacuation routes

Preparedness

Assignment of emergency management responsibilities
Emergency plans and possible hazards
Mutual aid agreements
Simulated-disaster exercises
Training for local government employees
Use of the Incident Command System

Response

Contributions and donations management
Damage assessment practices
Early-warning public notification systems
Emergency shelters and assistance
Evacuation practices
Geographic information systems
Medical services and equipment
On-site command and control
Public information and the news media

Recovery

Crime scene security
Crisis counseling
Disaster assistance to property owners and citizens
Management of fatalities
Rebuilding private structures and spaces
Restoration of public infrastructure and open spaces

---

availability, and location of their training programs. Many of these programs are provided free of charge, or for a limited cost, to local government officials.

U.S. Homeland Security Advisory System In 2002, Thomas Ridge, the Director of the Office of Homeland Security (now the secretary of the new department), set forth a national system of advising all levels of government—federal, state, and local—as well as the American people of the risk of a terrorist attack (see selection 23). Under this color-coded system, five levels of possible terrorist threats confronting the nation are specified: low (green), guarded (blue), elevated (yellow), high (orange), and severe (red). This alerting system spells out "protective measures" suited to each warning category.

Threat assessment   To assess the threat of terrorist acts by individuals or groups within their jurisdiction, cities and counties must work with state and federal agencies. Possible targets, both public and private, must be examined and ranked by level of risk. Appropriate safeguards should be made according to this ranking process. This comprehensive approach to emergency management fits well with FEMA's Integrated Emergency Management System (IEMS), which provides the framework for an all-hazard approach to emergency preparedness.

Building design and physical structures to improve public safety   Certain types of construction are more likely to withstand a terrorist attack than others (see selection 11). High-quality sprinkler systems and new fireproof roofing materials can reduce the chance of fire. Legal limits on building heights and building setback requirements also can lessen potential damage from attacks. These and other safety features should be incorporated into the design of new buildings. Physical structures also can be used to protect existing buildings. The selected placement of steel and concrete barriers around public buildings is frequently used to restrict vehicular access. Fences, walls, and other protective encasements can also be constructed. New types of devices and barriers are emerging in the marketplace that restrict access—both vehicular and pedestrian—to public buildings, monuments, and parks.

Municipal and county building codes   City and county building officials may want to update their codes for certain types of buildings—both public and private—to make them less vulnerable to terrorist attacks. The loss of life and property can be limited by retrofitting existing buildings or—sometimes a less expensive option—by building new structures that meet state-of-the-art safety criteria. Local government regulations should require the posting in buildings of exit signs, evacuation routes, and other appropriate security and safety information for the public.

Nonstructural measures to improve building safety   The use of police or security guards (depending on whether a building is public or private), metal detectors, and surveillance cameras can help protect the occupants of buildings by identifying possible threats. Police or security guards can inspect the personal belongings of people as they enter. Existing labor agreements, possibly state laws, will determine whether sworn police officers, civilian employees, or private security services are used for this purpose.

Pedestrian and vehicular evacuation routes   To ensure that the public can be evacuated from buildings in an effective and timely manner, local public safety officials should prepare building evacuation procedures. The safest and most expeditious exit routes from all buildings, especially those in high-risk areas, should be clearly explained. Buildings that are most vulnerable to a terrorist act may need specialized instructions for the public in case they must be evacuated. Vehicular evacuation routes leading out of town from urban centers should also be made available to the public. Depending on the type and size of a particular disaster, local officials may wish to issue a directive encouraging residents to evacuate their families to safer areas.

Preparedness

Assignment of emergency management responsibilities   All departments and agencies should be assigned specific duties to undertake in case of an emergency or disaster, whether of a human or natural cause. The roles of public safety, health, and public works employees have been redefined and enhanced to improve the nation's preparedness for a wide variety of terrorist activities. The proper roles for police and fire department personnel in the event of a disaster must be clearly defined beforehand. In case of a HAZMAT emergency, it is common for police to secure the perimeter of the area, while fire personnel deal with the hazardous materials. Other departmental employees would be called as needed to respond to different facets of an emergency.

Emergency plans and possible hazards   The emergency plans of cities and counties should include preparedness procedures for all types of likely disasters. These plans should detail the technical expertise that might be needed in the event of a terrorist attack, required resources, and the proper procedures to request assistance from neighboring jurisdictions as well as higher levels of government. Increasing emphasis must be placed on the interactions of local, state, and federal officials. Cities and counties with sites that might be prime targets of terrorists, such as nuclear power plants and busy ports, should include these sites in local emergency plans.

Mutual aid agreements   Fire departments have typically had mutual aid agreements with neighboring communities, but law enforcement, public works, and health departments are increasingly making these agreements as well. Mutual aid agreements ensure a prompt response by departments and agencies from contiguous municipal and county governments. The goal is a seamless response to an emergency once local resources have been exhausted. Under these agreements, a local government does not need to seek formal approval to use services from a neighboring jurisdiction, since the provision of requested services would be automatic. Since a terrorist act might affect more than one community, mutual aid agreements should be made with all contiguous communities, as well as the county in which a city or town is located. Contiguous counties should also have mutual aid agreements. Although states typically call upon the federal government when their resources have been exhausted, they can also benefit from such mutual aid agreements. Especially in geographic areas such as New England, where many small states exist, mutual aid agreements between contiguous states can help limit the loss of life and property for citizens during an emergency.

Simulated-disaster exercises   By organizing simulated-disaster exercises, local governments can help prepare for emergencies regardless of their cause. New preparedness procedures and techniques not only must be learned; they also must become fully operational. To become standard practice for public agencies—public safety, health, and public works—local plans must be tested. Simulated-disaster exercises help ensure that a local government's emergency operations plans hold up against events in the real world. Exercises should involve federal and state as well as local government agencies. Nongovernmental agencies from the nonprofit sector, hospitals, and assistance organizations also should participate. Emergency exercises give local officials the valuable opportunity to work the "bugs" out of their plans. Officials also can learn from their mistakes and adapt their plans accordingly. By improving preparedness, disaster exercises help to limit the loss of life and property once a real disaster takes place.

Training for local government employees   Since the September 11, 2001, terrorist incidents, specialized training programs have become available for public safety personnel and other local government employees in several areas relating to man-made disasters. Training programs are emerging in the areas of stress management for public safety employees, the management of fatalities, proper responses to weapons of mass destruction, intelligence and information networking, medical service readiness, and the provision of social services to victims of a disaster. Hazardous materials identification and modern decontamination practices are new to the training agenda. Many of these training programs are provided free of charge by state and federal government agencies. The selection on federal assistance programs highlights many of these grant-funded training programs.

Use of the Incident Command System (ICS)   The Federal Emergency Management Agency recommends the use of the ICS when local governments respond to natural and man-made emergencies. This system of management best accommodates a response by multiple actors, including state, federal, and local agencies. It gives the responsibility for command to an on-site manager, who reports to the emergency operations center. The use of this emergency management process allows for the immediate coordination of services from numerous sources, including other levels of government. Local governments that use the ICS enhance their effectiveness, streamline their chain of command, and eliminate the possible duplication of services. State governments and the federal government provide much needed and valuable training in the use of this contemporary and state-of-the-art emergency management technique.

Response

Contributions and donations management   In large-scale man-made or natural disasters, private citizens and local community organizations step forward to help local victims and their families. As the response of New York City to the World Trade Center attack demonstrated, nonprofit organizations, as well as members of the public, are eager to donate goods and services and lend assistance to others during a disaster. Specific requests can be made by public officials if specialized equipment or services are needed. Locations should be designated, and an accurate accounting should be kept of those groups and individuals who donate goods and services during or after an emergency. Collection of these contributions from the private and nonprofit sectors should be managed so as not to interfere in any way with the professional response by police and fire personnel, or other departments involved in a response.

Damage assessment practices   Damage assessment at the local level must be accurate and immediate, since assistance from higher levels of government depends on this information. Appropriate municipal and county officials must be trained in the details of this emergency management function. In large jurisdictions, teams of employees are usually assigned to cover different neighborhoods, or areas, of a city or county after a disaster occurs. As a local government's response unfolds, the information on damage that is gathered must be continually verified and reassessed to ensure its accuracy. Procedures should exist in advance to properly document the damage done to real property, as well as methods to determine the financial magnitude of such damage.

Early-warning public notification systems   A key feature of a local government's response to an emergency is prompt notification of the public. In the case of a flood, for example, authorities may have several hours' lead time in which to warn the public. In the case of a terrorist act, the warning to the public must be as immediate as circumstances allow. Reverse 911 notification systems are prompt and flexible enough to issue a warning to citizens on a block-by-block or a neighborhood-by-neighborhood basis. Traditional means of notifying citizens, such as the public media, may not be readily available because of the time of day or night that an incident occurs. Citywide sirens (some have voice-over capability) might then be used to inform the public. Government-access cable television channels can also be used for this purpose, but not as a primary source of information, since the warning would not reach all of the citizens in the community.

Emergency shelters and assistance   A natural or man-made disaster, especially a carefully designed terrorist attack, could leave a large number of citizens without food, water, and shelter. Emergency shelters (beds and restrooms) and assistance (food, water, and first-aid stations) would be needed immediately. The location and size of such shelters and the organizations that would provide assistance must be known in advance of an emergency. Usually public buildings are used for this purpose, with assistance provided by the Red Cross and Salvation Army. Municipal or county employees, depending upon the state and its local forms of government, may provide health assistance. In case primary facilities are damaged, a comprehensive emergency operations plan should note the location of appropriate back-up facilities.

Evacuation practices   In the case of an arson fire or bombing, people must be evacuated immediately from all impacted buildings and surrounding areas. Procedures should exist to facilitate the smooth evacuation of large numbers of people in the shortest time possible. In the case of fire or the imminent collapse of a building, a prompt response could save many lives. Vehicles, such as buses or vans, owned by the local government should be used to facilitate evacuation. The number of vehicles available, as well as issues related to accessibility, should be worked out in advance of an incident. Proper exit signs and evacuation routes should be properly posted in all buildings, both public and private. The location of safety equipment and first aid supplies should also be posted.

Geographic information systems (GIS)   Computerized mapping using geographic information systems (GIS) can provide immediate assistance to local governments in their response to either natural or man-made disasters. Cities and counties should know the location of public utilities, public telephones, power grids, public open spaces, hospitals, natural amenities, and other useful information in their electronic database. This is in addition to the usual information, such as the location of property lines and buildings. Staging areas, incident command posts, emergency shelters, designated medical facilities, and approved evacuation routes should be plotted for use by city and county employees when responding to emergencies. The use of GIS was critical in New York City's response to the September 2001 terrorist attack and helped police officers and firefighters save lives.

Medical services and equipment   The availability of all medical services and equipment should be known in advance of an incident. The locations of hospitals, ambulance companies, and private medical providers—and the resources they can provide—must be included in emergency operations plans. Because primary facilities may be incapacitated during a disaster, back-up medical facilities and services should also be known and determined in advance. Also needed are decontamination procedures to be followed in the event of a chemical or biological incident. Public information must also be provided within a short time frame to relatives and friends of victims. Careful advance planning in these critical areas can lead to a timely and professional response by local government personnel.

On-site command and control   As the discussion of the Incident Command System in the section on preparedness made clear, on-site management of a disaster is essential. The on-site manager and command staff are responsible for coordinating the response, including the interaction of public officials for various agencies (for example, city, county, state, federal, and nonprofit). The on-site command staff would report to the emergency operations center, which would relay incident information to the appropriate people, including elected officials and the news media. Responders (police and fire personnel and others) report their findings to incident commanders, who coordinate the immediate on-scene response. The location of main command sites and back-up sites should be determined on a neighborhood basis before an incident occurs. A site where an act of terrorism has taken place should be treated like a crime scene. This requires extra security and investigative services provided by police personnel.

Public information and the news media   Although local and state news media pay attention to typical natural disasters at first, their interest, as well as that of the public, soon wanes. In the case of a man-made disaster, such as an act of terrorism, news media (print and broadcast) at all levels (local, state, and national) will very likely have a keen interest in a local government's response for some time. It is essential to have someone at the emergency operations center who is knowledgeable about what happened and accessible to the media. The media can offer an excellent way for local government officials to issue warnings and evacuation notices to the public. The media should be kept away from the epicenter of a local disaster whenever possible. Representatives of the news media should not be allowed to get through the perimeter security of an incident. Proper security measures must be provided by police personnel to achieve this goal.

Recovery

Crime scene security   Man-made disasters such as terrorist acts are crimes, and the location of the incident should be treated as a crime scene, as noted earlier. Evidence at the site must be secured, collected, and protected for future use in legal proceedings. This evidence may be used to prosecute the perpetrators at a later date, once the recovery phase of the emergency response has been completed. This means that public access to the site must be limited. First responders must be trained by law enforcement personnel to both identify and protect evidence at the site of the disaster. Debris removal must be undertaken under special, and controlled, circumstances. Depending on the size of a disaster, this process could take weeks, even months, to complete.

Crisis counseling   Following a disaster, public safety employees, and citizens in general, often suffer a variety of stress-related symptoms, including anger, depression, headaches, and insomnia. Debriefings of affected personnel by experienced counselors should take place as soon as possible after a disaster (see selections 19 and 20). Psychologists, chaplains, family counselors, and mental health professionals typically provide these services. Many employee assistance programs (EAPs) offer counseling services to city and county employees. If a jurisdiction does not have an EAP program in place, it may need to hire trained specialists to provide postdisaster counseling services to victims and their families. Ideally, these services should be provided within 24 to 48 hours after an emergency takes place.

Disaster assistance to property owners and citizens   Public officials in the jurisdiction where a natural or man-made disaster occurs should establish a clearinghouse to coordinate assistance to victims and their families. The Federal Emergency Management Agency, state governments, the Red Cross, and other nonprofit organizations frequently offer this type of assistance. By providing a centralized location for assistance information, a local government will be able to speed up the process of restoring order after a disaster. It is incumbent upon local officials to inform the public about the disaster assistance programs that are available—and to coordinate these programs. Local government officials may wish to provide for "gap" coverage to property owners and citizens who were victims of a disaster.

Management of fatalities   The limited scope of most local disasters does not require extensive planning for the management of on-site fatalities. In the case of terrorist incidents, however, local government officials may need to make arrangements for temporary morgues (see selection 21). Local mortuaries must also be put on alert to handle the additional deaths created by these disasters. Procedures for promptly notifying victims' next-of-kin must be worked out. Emergency operations plans must include a section pertaining to the management of on-site fatalities. It is prudent to include this information in all local emergency response plans, regardless of the size of the jurisdiction involved. Resources for the management of fatalities are an integral part of the recovery phase of a local government's emergency management plan.

Rebuilding private structures and spaces   Typically, after a natural disaster, the owner of the damaged property will file a claim with his or her insurance company. Once the monetary settlement is received, the owner can begin reconstruction. In the case of a terrorist attack causing widespread damage, the local government has an important role to play in the rebuilding process. Local officials must notify all owners of damaged property and ask them to clear their land, ensure it is free of hazards, properly fence it for public safety purposes, and, ultimately, reconstruct buildings on the cleared property. It may be in the public's interest for local government officials to perform some of these tasks. In this case, permission should be sought from property owners. Public officials may seek title to impacted private properties if an aggregation of individual ownerships best serves the public interest. This especially holds true if local owners of commercial and residential properties do not want to rebuild in the disaster area.

Restoration of public infrastructure and open spaces   After a disaster, citizens expect local public officials to restore public infrastructure (for example, sewer and water lines, electricity, roadways, sidewalks, and public transit) and public open spaces (parks, playgrounds, walkways, bikeways, trails, beach access, and waterways) in a timely manner. While the public sector must hold the private sector accountable for the restoration of private property, citizens should hold their local government officials accountable for the restoration of public property. City and county officials should take prompt action to merit citizens' trust in this regard.

Conclusion

Historical events at home and abroad have shaped the way U.S. citizens and all levels of government have prepared for emergencies. During and immediately after World War II, the phrase *civil defense* became commonplace throughout the nation. Under this heading, numerous practices and techniques were developed, primarily by the federal government, to protect citizens in case of attack or invasion by military forces from other countries, particularly the Soviet Union during the postwar arms race. During the *Cold War*, when more nations sought the capability to produce nuclear bombs, the nature of civil defense changed to include safeguards to protect citizens in case of a nuclear attack. Then, as the Cold War waned and finally ended in the early 1990s with the collapse of the Soviet Union and the reunification of Germany, more sophisticated practices evolved under the general heading of *emergency management*. Natural disasters, rather than man-made ones, dominated emergency management at the end of the twentieth century. How to cope with tornadoes, hurricanes, floods, ice storms, and the like, and the damage they brought, became the main concern of local emergency response plans. The preoccupation with natural disasters remained the main focus of emergency management for a number of years.

After the terrorist attacks in New York City and the Pentagon in September 2001, and the hijacking that led to the crash in rural Pennsylvania, the federal government coined the phrase *homeland security* to describe actions taken at all levels of government to protect citizens from future acts of violence by terrorists. While the emergency management practices and techniques that evolve during the coming years will be different from the civil defense measures of the fifties and sixties, the goal of these initiatives is still the same: to limit the loss of life and property during a disaster. This goal requires the implementation of policies and the testing of procedures in the four phases of emergency management discussed throughout this volume. The Federal Emergency Management Agency's all-hazard approach to emergency management enables local government officials to prepare comprehensive plans that encompass all potential hazards, both natural and man-made. The field of emergency management has gone full circle in the past half-century. As in the 1950s, external threats are focusing the attention of emergency planners on man-made disasters. At the same time, plans to cope with natural disasters continue.

Local government officials—both elected and appointed—are taking seriously the dangers posed by terrorists, and they are implementing the practices discussed in this volume, and other measures, to meet this threat. Secretary Ridge in March 2003 announced that nearly $600 million has been made available to assist state and local public safety and law enforcement personnel in their efforts to prevent, prepare for, and respond to terrorism. In the early twenty-first century, the discipline of emergency management is in the spotlight, and it is rapidly expanding in new directions. For example, the Naval Postgraduate School in Monterey, California, has developed the nation's first master's degree program in Security Studies with a specialization in Homeland Security. New emergency management practices will be envisioned, developed, promulgated, tested, and standardized at all levels of government in the years ahead. Those presented in this volume are at the promising forefront of these developments.

In September 2001, terrorists' calculated acts of violence on U.S. soil shattered a sense of security that American citizens had felt for many years. Additional governmental safeguards and security measures became an urgent necessity in response to these events. Public officials and citizens are now re-examining the proper balance between the need for public safety measures and individual civil liberties. No doubt a national debate will evolve as these new safeguards and security measures are reviewed and discussed in the U.S. Congress, in state capitals, and in city halls throughout the nation. In this national debate, city and county managers and other leaders of local government will have an important voice.

About the editor and contributors

Editor

Roger L. Kemp, Ph.D., has been a city manager on both the West and the East Coasts for over two decades. He is presently city manager of Meriden, Connecticut, the second largest city in the state with the council-manager form of government. Dr. Kemp has also been an adjunct professor over the years at such major educational institutions as the University of California, Golden Gate University, Rutgers University, and the University of Connecticut. He holds a B.S. degree in business administration, both M.P.A. and M.B.A. degrees, and a Ph.D. degree in public administration, and is a graduate of the Program for Senior Executives in State and Local Government, John F. Kennedy School of Government, Harvard University. Roger is president (2002–2003) of the Connecticut Town and City Management Association (CTCMA), and is the immediate past-president of the Connecticut chapter of the American Society for Public Administration (ASPA). He has written and edited numerous books and articles on various topics related to municipal management. Dr. Kemp received the designation of *ICMA Credentialed Manager* in 2002.

Contributors

Following are the affiliations of the contributors at the time the articles were written.

David R. Blossom, vice chair, Fire and Life Safety Code Board of Adjustments and Appeals, Orange County, Florida; and member, Building and Fire Code Appeals Board, Orlando, Florida.

D. Douglas Bodrero, senior executive and manager, State and Local Anti-Terrorism Training Program, Institute for Intergovernmental Research, Tallahassee, Florida.

Ben Canada, analyst in American national government, Government and Finance Division, Congressional Research Service, Library of Congress, Washington, D.C.

Ed Comeau, former fire protection engineer, Fire Department, Phoenix, Arizona.

Chris DeChant, firefighter and paramedic, Fire Department, Glendale, Arizona.

Dave Douglas, sergeant, Police Department, San Diego, California.

Timothy Elliott, contributing editor, *Homeland Protection Professional*, A.J. Parrino & Associates, Ltd., Western Springs, Illinois.

Bill Flynt, lieutenant colonel, U.S. Army, Fort Leavenworth, Kansas.

Rickey Hargrave, police chaplain, Police Department, McKinney, Texas.

Matthew J. Hickman, statistician, Bureau of Justice Statistics, U.S. Department of Justice, Washington, D.C.

Russ Johnson, public safety manager, ESRI, Redlands, California.

Dennis Labriola, president, Admit Computer Services, Farmingdale, New York.

Randall D. Larson, dispatch supervisor and field communications manager, Fire Department, San José, California.

Philip M. McVey, deputy sheriff, County of Los Angeles, California.

John Nicholson, associate editor, *NFPA Journal*, National Fire Protection Association, Quincy, Massachusetts.

Ron Olin, chief of police, Lawrence, Kansas.

Gary Raymer, chief of police, Bowling Green, Kentucky.

Brian A. Reaves, chief statistician, Law Enforcement and Pretrial Statistics, Bureau of Justice Statistics, U.S. Department of Justice, Washington, D.C.

Thomas Ridge, secretary, Department of Homeland Security, Washington, D.C.

Jeffrey W. Runge, administrator, National Highway Traffic Safety Administration, U.S. Department of Transportation, Washington, D.C.

James Russo, chief of police, Hempstead, New York.

Robert L. Smith, lieutenant, Stress Management Unit, Fire Department, Washington Township, Indianapolis, Indiana.

Beth Wade, managing editor, *American City & County*, PRIMEDIA Business Magazines & Media, Inc., Overland Park, Kansas.

David Wagman, freelance writer, Denver, Colorado.

Janet Ward, senior editor, *Homeland Protection Professional*, A.J. Parrino & Associates, Ltd., Western Springs, Illinois.

Rick Wimberly, public safety director, Dialogue Communications Corporation, Franklin, Tennessee.

Appendices

Appendix A

Terrorism preparedness and response

FEMA's mission

To reduce loss of life and property and protect our institutions from all hazards by leading and supporting the Nation in a comprehensive, risk-based emergency management program of mitigation, preparedness, response, and recovery.

FEMA's terrorism mission

FEMA supports local, State, and Federal governments in preparing for and responding to terrorism using unique consequence management authorities, responsibilities, and capabilities.

FEMA's role in terrorism preparedness and response

Presidential Decision Directive (PDD)—39 and PDD—62: U.S. Policy on Counterterrorism

These two PDD's state that the United States will have the ability to respond rapidly and decisively to terrorism and are the basis for FEMA's domestic preparedness and response activities for consequence management in response to terrorist incidents involving Weapons of Mass Destruction (WMD).

Federal Response Plan (FRP)

The FRP established a process and structure for the systematic, coordinated, and effective delivery of Federal assistance to address the consequences of any major disaster or emergency declared under the Robert T. Stafford Disaster Relief and Emergency Assistance Act.

Terrorism Incident Annex

The FRP Terrorism Incident Annex, created in 1999, defines the structures to coordinate crisis management with consequence management. The Annex:

- Supplements the FRP with special considerations for terrorism response.
- Supports PDD's to establish policy to respond to terrorism.
- Describes linkages between crisis management and consequence management activities before, during, and after an event.
- Describes responsibilities of Federal agencies to provide support for technical response operations.

Source: Joe M. Allbaugh, Federal Emergency Management Agency (FEMA), Federal Central Plaza, 500 C Street, S.W., Washington, D.C. 20472 (Brochure L255 dated March 2001). Mr. Allbaugh is director of FEMA.

State and Local Guide (SLG)—101

Chapter 6, Hazard—Unique Planning Considerations, Attachment G—Terrorism, was developed to aide State and local emergency managers in developing and maintaining a consequence management plan for preparing for and responding to a terrorist incident.

FEMA sponsored training

Emergency Management Institute

FEMA provides training at the Emergency Management Institute for State and local emergency management officials. Some of the terrorism related training includes

- Emergency Response to Criminal and Terrorist Incidents.
- Integrated Emergency Management Course—Consequences of Terrorism.
- Mass Facilities Incident Course.
- Senior Officials Workshop.

National Fire Academy

FEMA also provides on-site and off-site training via the National Fire Academy for first responders. Training includes

- Tactical Considerations—Company Officer/Emergency Medical Services/Hazardous Materials
- Strategic Considerations for Command Officers.
- Emergency Response to Terrorism: Basic Concepts/Incident Management.
- Emergency Response to Terrorism: Self Study

Rapid Response Information System (RRIS)

The RRIS is a Federal interagency program established and maintained by FEMA. The RRIS provides immediate access to information for response to a WMD terrorism incident. Information available on the RRIS includes

- Federal capabilities that could be made available to State and local communities in response to an incident involving WMD.
- Information on selected WMD equipment and General Services Administration (GSA) excess/surplus property.
- Database on chemical and biological warfare agents with information on characteristics and safety precautions.
- Database of radiological materials with information on physical characteristics and safety precautions.
- A listing of reference documents available on the Internet.
- A listing of Federal WMD training courses.

FEMA grants to State and local entities

Funding is provided to State and local entities through the Terrorism Consequence Management Preparedness Assistance (TCMPA) Program via the Emergency Management Performance Grant (EMPG) Program. Funding may be used to enhance terrorism preparedness through planning, training, and exercises.

Federal assistance and resources

What Federal assistance can be provided?

- Immediate response for lifesaving and life-protecting needs.
- Planning, training, and exercises.
- Support of disaster operations.
- Restoration, repair, or replacement of public services and facilities.
- Mitigate or lessen the effects of a disaster in the future.

What Federal resources can be provided?

- Emergency response teams.
- Emergency support teams.
- Specialized teams for
  - Rapid assessment
  - Agent detection
  - Decontamination
  - Emergency communications
  - Medical assistance and support
  - Urban search and rescue activities
  - Emergency power restoration
  - Incident management
  - Community management

Appendix B

Federal disaster declaration process

(1) Disaster event, either man-made or natural, occurs.

(2) Local/State officials assess damage.

(3) Governor reviews damage reports and decides to seek Federal help.

(4) Governor asks FEMA regional office to participate in Federal/State preliminary damage assessments (PDAs).

(5) Joint FEMA/State PDAs conducted.

(6) Governor requests a Federal disaster declaration through its FEMA regional office.

(7) Regional office reviews request and sends its recommendation to FEMA headquarters.

(8) FEMA officials in Washington, D.C., prepare a declaration packet, review information, and recommend approving or denying the request.

(9) FEMA director reviews the declaration packet and sends a recommendation for approval or denial to the President.

(10) President makes final determination on Federal disaster declaration.

Source: Federal Emergency Management Agency (FEMA), Federal Center Plaza, 500 C Street, S.W., Washington, D.C. 20472.

Appendix C

Federal Emergency Management Agency regional offices

FEMA Region I
442 J.W. McCormack
POCH
Boston, MA 02109
(617) 223-9540

FEMA Region II
26 Federal Plaza
New York, NY 10278
(212) 680-3600

FEMA Region III
One Independence Mall, Sixth Floor
615 Chestnut Street
Philadelphia, PA 19106
(215) 931-5608

FEMA Region IV
3003 Chamblee-Tucker Road
Atlanta, GA 30341
(770) 220-5200

FEMA Region V
536 South Clark Street, Sixth Floor
Chicago, IL 60605
(312) 408-5500

FEMA Region VI
Federal Regional Center
800 North Loop 288
Denton, TX 76209
(940) 898-5399

FEMA Region VII
2323 Grand Boulevard, Suite 900
Kansas City, MO 64108
(816) 283-7061

FEMA Region VIII
Federal Center
Building 710, Box 25267
Denver, CO 80225
(303) 235-4800

FEMA Region IX
1111 Broadway, Suite 1200
Oakland, CA 94607
(515) 627-7100

FEMA Region X
Federal Regional Center
130 228th Street, S.W.
Bothell, WA 98021
(425) 487-4600

Source: Federal Emergency Management Agency (FEMA), Federal Center Plaza, 500 C Street, S.W., Washington, D.C. 20472; http://www.fema.gov./regions/index.shtm.

Appendix D

State offices and agencies of emergency management

A

Alabama Emergency Management
    Agency
5898 County Road 41
P.O. Drawer 2160
Clanton, Alabama 35046-2160
(205) 280-2200
(205) 280-2495 FAX
http://www.aema.state.al.us

Alaska Division of Emergency Services
P.O. Box 5750
Fort Richardson, Alaska 99505-5750
(907) 428-7000
(907) 428-7009 FAX
http://www.ak-prepared.com

American Samoa Territorial Emergency
    Management Coordination
    (TEMCO)
American Samoa Government
P.O. Box 1086
Pago Pago, American Samoa 96799
(011)(684) 699-6415
(011)(684) 699-6414 FAX

Arizona Division of Emergency
    Management
5636 East McDowell Road
Phoenix, Arizona 85008
(602) 244-0504 or 1-800-411-2336
http://www.dem.state.az.us

Arkansas Department of Emergency
    Management
P.O. Box 758
Conway, Arkansas 72033
(501) 730-9750
(501) 730-9754 FAX
http://www.adem.state.ar.us

C

California Governor's Office of
    Emergency Services
3650 Schriever Avenue
Mather, CA 95655
(916) 845-8400
http://www.oes.ca.gov

Colorado Office of Emergency
    Management
Division of Local Government
Department of Local Affairs
15075 South Golden Road
Golden, Colorado 80401-3979
(303) 273-1622
(303) 273-1795 FAX
www.dola.state.co.us/oem/
    oemindex.htm

Connecticut Office of Emergency
    Management
Military Department
360 Broad Street
Hartford, Connecticut 06105
(860) 566-3180
(860) 247-0664 FAX
http://www.mil.state.ct.us/oem.htm

Source: Federal Emergency Management Agency (FEMA), Federal Center Plaza, 500 C Street, S.W., Washington, D.C. 20472; http://www.fema.gov/fema/statedr.shtm.

D

Delaware Emergency Management
   Agency
165 Brick Store Landing Road
Smyrna, Delaware 19977
(302) 659-3362
(302) 659-6855 FAX
http://www.state.de.us/dema/index.htm

District of Columbia Emergency
   Management Agency
2000 14th Street, N.W., Eighth Floor
Washington, D.C. 20009
(202) 727-6161
(202) 673-2290 FAX
http://www.dcema.dc.gov

F

Florida Division of Emergency
   Management
2555 Shumard Oak Boulevard
Tallahassee, Florida 32399-2100
(850) 413-9969
(850) 488-1016 FAX
http://www.floridadisaster.org

G

Georgia Emergency
   Management Agency
P.O. Box 18055
Atlanta, Georgia 30316-0055
(404) 635-7000
(404) 635-7205 FAX
http://www.state.ga.us/gema

Office of Civil Defense
Government of Guam
P.O. Box 2877
Hagatna, Guam 96932
(011)(671) 475-9600
(011)(671) 477-3727 FAX
http://ns.gov.gu

H

Hawaii State Civil Defense
3949 Diamond Head Road
Honolulu, Hawaii 96816-4495
(808) 733-4300
(808) 733-4287 FAX
http://www.scd.state.hi.us

I

Idaho Bureau of Disaster Services
4040 Guard Street, Building 600
Boise, Idaho 83705-5004
(208) 334-3460
(208) 334-2322 FAX
http://www2.state.id.us/bds

Illinois Emergency Management Agency
110 East Adams Street
Springfield, Illinois 62701
(217) 782-2700
(217) 524-7967 FAX
http://www.state.il.us/iema

Indiana State Emergency Management
   Agency
302 West Washington Street
Room E-208 A
Indianapolis, Indiana 46204-2767
(317) 232-3986
(317) 232-3895 FAX
http://www.ai.org/sema/index.html

Iowa Division of Emergency
   Management
Department of Public Defense
Hoover Office Building
Des Moines, Iowa 50319
(515) 281-3231
http://www.state.ia.us/government/
   dpd/emd/index.htm

K

Kansas Division of Emergency
   Management
2800 S.W. Topeka Boulevard
Topeka, Kansas 66611-1287
(785) 274-1401
(785) 274-1426 FAX
http://www.ink.org/public/kdem

Kentucky Emergency Management
EOC Building
100 Minuteman Parkway, Building 100
Frankfort, Kentucky 40601-6168
(502) 607-1682
(502) 607-1614 FAX
http://kyem.dma.state.ky.us

L

Louisiana Office of Emergency
  Preparedness
7667 Independence Boulevard
Baton Rouge, Louisiana 70806
(225) 925-7500
(225) 925-7501 FAX
http://www.loep.state.la.us

M

Maine Emergency Management Agency
State Office Building, Station 72
Augusta, Maine 04333
(207) 626-4503
(207) 626-4499 FAX
http://www.state.me.us/mema/
  memahome.htm

CNMI Emergency Management Office
Office of the Governor
Commonwealth of the Northern
  Mariana Islands
P.O. Box 10007
Saipan, Mariana Islands 96950
(670) 322-9529
(670) 322-7743 FAX
http://www.cnmiemo.org

National Disaster Management Office
Office of the Chief Secretary
P.O. Box 15
Majuro, Republic of the Marshall
  Islands 96960-0015
(011)(692) 625-5181
(011)(692) 625-6896 FAX

Maryland Emergency Management
  Agency
Camp Fretterd Military Reservation
5401 Rue Saint Lo Drive
Reisterstown, Maryland 21136
(410) 517-3600
(877) 636-2872 Toll Free
(410) 517-3610 FAX
http://www.mema.state.md.us

Massachusetts Emergency
  Management Agency
400 Worcester Road
Framingham, Massachusetts
  01702-5399
(508) 820-2000
(508) 820-2030 FAX
http://www.state.ma.us/mema

Michigan Division of Emergency
  Management
4000 Collins Road
P.O. Box 30636
Lansing, Michigan 48909-8136
(517) 333-5042
(517) 333-4987 FAX
http://www.msp.state.mi.us/
  division/emd/emdweb1.htm

National Disaster Control Officer
Federated States of Micronesia
P.O. Box PS-53
Kolonia, Pohnpei, Micronesia 96941
(011)(691) 320-8815
(001)(691) 320-2785 FAX

Minnesota Division of Emergency
  Management
Department of Public Safety
Suite 223
444 Cedar Street
St. Paul, Minnesota 55101-6223
(615) 297-7372
(615) 269-0459 FAX
http://www.dps.state.mn.us/emermgt

Mississippi Emergency Management
  Agency
P.O. Box 4501, Fondren Station
Jackson, Mississippi 39296-4501
(601) 352-9100
(800) 442-6362 Toll Free
(601) 352-8314 FAX
http://www.mema.state.ms.us
http://www.memaorg.com

Missouri Emergency Management
  Agency
P.O. Box 16
2302 Militia Drive
Jefferson City, Missouri 65102
(573) 526-9100
(573) 634-7966 FAX
http://www.sema.state.mo.us/
  semapage.htm

Montana Division of Disaster &
  Emergency Services
1900 Williams Street
P.O. Box 4789
Helena, Montana 59604-4789
(406) 841-3911
(406) 444-3965 FAX
http://www.state.mt.us/dma/des/
  index.shtml

N

Nebraska Emergency Management
  Agency
1300 Military Road
Lincoln, Nebraska 68508-1090
(402) 471-7421
(402) 471-7433 FAX
http://www.nebema.org

Nevada Division of Emergency
  Management
2525 South Carson Street
Carson City, Nevada 89711
(775) 687-4240
(775) 687-6788 FAX
http://dem.state.nv.us

Governor's Office of Emergency
  Management
State Office Park South
107 Pleasant Street
Concord, New Hampshire 03301
(603) 271-2231
(603) 225-7341 FAX
http://www.nhoem.state.nh.us

New Jersey Office of Emergency
  Management
Emergency Management Bureau
P.O. Box 7068
West Trenton, New Jersey 08628-0068
(609) 538-6050 Monday-Friday
(609) 882-2000 ext. 6311 (24/7)
(609) 538-0345 FAX
http://www.state.nj.us/oem/county

New Mexico Department
  of Public Safety
Office of Emergency Services
  and Security
13 Bataan Boulevard
P.O. Box 1628
Santa Fe, New Mexico 87505
(505) 476-9600
(505) 476-9695 FAX
http://www.dps.nm.org/emergency/
  index.htm

Emergency Management Bureau
Department of Public Safety
13 Bataan Boulevard
P.O. Box 1628
Santa Fe, New Mexico 87505
(505) 476-9606
(505) 476-9650 FAX
http://www.dps.nm.org/emc.htm

New York State Emergency
  Management Office
1220 Washington Avenue
Building 2, Suite 101
Albany, New York 12226-2251
(518) 457-2222
(518) 457-9995 FAX
http://www.nysemo.state.ny.us

North Carolina Division of
  Emergency Management
116 West Jones Street
Raleigh, North Carolina 27603
(919) 733-3867
(919) 733-5406 FAX
http://www.dem.dcc.state.nc.us

North Dakota Division of
  Emergency Management
P.O. Box 5511
Bismarck, North Dakota 58506-5511
(701) 328-8100
(701) 328-8181 FAX
http://www.state.nd.us/dem

O

Ohio Emergency Management Agency
2855 West Dublin Granville Road
Columbus, Ohio 43235-2206
(614) 889-7150
(614) 889-7183 FAX
http://www.state.oh.us/odps/division/
  ema

Office of Civil Emergency Management
2401 N. Lincoln Boulevard, Suite C51
Oklahoma City, Oklahoma 73152
(405) 521-2481
(405) 521-4053 FAX
http://www.odcem.state.ok.us

Oregon Emergency Management
Department of State Police
3225 State Street
Salem, Oregon 97301
(503) 378-2911
(503) 588-1378
http://www.osp.state.or.us/oem

P

Palau NEMO Coordinator
Office of the President
P.O. Box 100
Koror, Republic of Palau 96940
(011)(680) 488-2422
(011)(680) 488-3312

Pennsylvania Emergency
    Management Agency
P.O. Box 3321
Harrisburg, Pennsylvania 17105-3321
(717) 651-2001
(717) 651-2040 FAX
http://www.pema.state.pa.us

Puerto Rico Emergency Management
    Agency
P.O. Box 966597
San Juan, Puerto Rico 00906-6597
(787) 724-0124
(787) 725-4244 FAX

R

Rhode Island Emergency
    Management Agency
645 New London Avenue
Cranston, Rhode Island 02920-3003
(401) 946-9996
(401) 944-1891 FAX
http://www.state.ri.us/riema/
    riemaaa.html

S

South Carolina Emergency
    Management Division
1100 Fish Hatchery Road
West Columbia, South Carolina 29172
(803) 737-8500
(803) 737-8570 FAX
http://www.state.sc.us/epd

South Dakota Division of Emergency
    Management
500 East Capitol
Pierre, South Dakota 57501-5070
(605) 773-3231
(605) 773-3580 FAX
http://www.state.sd.us/state/
    executive/military/sddem.htm

T

Tennessee Emergency Management
    Agency
3041 Sidco Drive
Nashville, Tennessee 37204-1502
(615) 741-4332
(615) 242-9635 FAX
http://www.tnema.org

Texas Department of Public Safety
Emergency Management Service
5805 North Lamar
Austin, Texas 78752
(512) 424-2138
(512) 424-2444 FAX
http://www.txdps.state.tx.us/dem

U

Utah Division of Emergency Services
    and Homeland Security
1110 State Office Building
P.O. Box 141710
Salt Lake City, Utah 84114-1710
(801) 538-3400
(801) 538-3770 FAX
http://www.des.utah.gov

V

Vermont Emergency Management
    Agency
Department of Public Safety
Waterbury State Complex
103 South Main Street
Waterbury, Vermont 05671-2101
(802) 244-8721
(802) 244-8655 FAX
http://www.dps.state.vt.us

Virgin Islands Territorial Emergency
    Management (VITEMA)
2-C Contant, A-Q Building
Virgin Islands 00820
(304) 774-2244
(304) 774-1491

Virginia Department of Emergency
    Management
10501 Trade Court
Richmond, VA 23236-3713
(804) 897-6502
(804) 897-6506
http://www.vdem.state.va.us

W

Washington Military Department
Emergency Management Division
Building 20, M/S: TA-20
Camp Murray, Washington 98430-5122
(253) 512-7000
(253) 512-7200 FAX
http://emd.wa.gov

West Virginia Office of
    Emergency Services
Building 1, Room EB-80
1900 Kanawha Boulevard, East
Charleston, West Virginia 25305-0360
(304) 558-5380
(304) 344-4538 FAX
http://www.state.wv.us/wvoes

Wisconsin Emergency Management
2400 Wright Street
Madison, Wisconsin 53704
(608) 242-3232
(608) 242-3247 FAX
http://badger.state.wi.us/agencies/dma/
    wem/index.htm

Wyoming Emergency Management
    Agency
5500 Bishop Boulevard
Cheyenne, Wyoming 82009-3320
(307) 777-4920
(307) 635-6017 FAX
http://wema.state.wy.us

Appendix E

Homeland security acronyms

AMS	Aerial Measuring System
ARAC	Atmospheric Release Advisory Capability
CBRN	Chemical/biological/radiation/nuclear
CB-RRT	Chemical and Biological Rapid Response Team
CDC	Centers for Disease Control
CEPPO	Chemical Emergency Preparedness and Prevention Office
CID	Criminal Investigations Division
DEST	Domestic Emergency Support Team
DHHS	Department of Health and Human Services
DOD	Department of Defense
DoE	Department of Energy
DoJ	Department of Justice
DMAT	Disaster Medical Assistance Team
EPA	Environmental Protection Agency
EPCRA	Environmental Protection & Community Right-to-Know Act
ERRS	Emergency and Rapid Response Team
ERT	Environmental Response Team
FBI	Federal Bureau of Investigation
FCC	Federal Coordination Center
FCO	Federal Coordinating Office
FEMA	Federal Emergency Management Agency
FRMAC	Federal Radiological Monitoring Assessment Center
HHS	Health and Human Services
JIC	Joint Information Center
JOC	Joint Operations Center
JTOT	Joint Technical Operations Team
LEO	Law Enforcement Online
LFA	Lead Federal Agency

LGAT	Lincoln Gold Augmentation Team
LEPC	Local Emergency Planning Committees
MMRS	Metropolitan Medical Response System
MMST	Metropolitan Medical Strike Team
MSU	Medical Support Units
NDMS	National Disaster Medical System
NDPO	National Domestic Preparedness Office
NEIC	National Enforcement Investigations Center
NEST	Nuclear Emergency Support Team
NRST	Nuclear Radiological Support Team
NRS	National Response System
NRT	National Response Team
OEP	Office of Emergency Preparedness
OERR	Office of Emergency and Remedial Response
ORIA	Office of Radiation and Indoor Air
OSC	On-Scene Coordinators
RAID	Rapid Assessment and Initial Detection
RAP	Radiation Assistance Program
REAC/TS	Radiation Emergency Assistance Center/Training Site
RERT	Radiological Emergency Response Team
ROC	Regional Operations Center
RRT	Regional Response Teams
SAC	Special Agent in Charge
SAT	Search Augmentation Team
SIOC	Strategic Information Operations Center
SRT	Search Response Team
START	Superfund Technical Assessment and Response Team
SSC	Scientific Support Coordinators
WMD	Weapons of Mass Destruction

Appendix F

Homeland security Internet resources

Agency for Toxic Substances and Disease Registry
U.S. Department of Health and Human Services
http://www.atsdr.cdc.gov/atsdrhome.html

American Institute of Architects
http://www.aia.org

American Red Cross
http://www.redcross.org

America Responds to Terrorism
Office of Citizen Services and Communications
U.S. General Services Administration
http://www.firstgov.gov

American Society of Civil Engineers
http://www.asce.org

ANSER Institute for Homeland Security
http://homelandsecurity.org

Bureau of Alcohol, Tobacco, and Firearms
U.S. Department of the Treasury
http://www.atf.treas.gov

Centers for Disease Control and Prevention
U.S. Department of Health and Human Services
http://www.cdc.gov

Chemical Emergency Preparedness and Prevention Office
Environmental Protection Agency
http://www.epa.gov/swercepp

Counterterrorism Office
U.S. Department of State
http://www.state.gov/s/ct

Domestic Terrorism Research Center
John F. Kennedy School of Government
Harvard University
http://www.ksg.harvard.edu/terrorism

Emergency Management Institute
Federal Emergency Management Agency
http://training.fema.gov/emiweb

Federal Bureau of Investigation
http://www.fbi.gov

Federal Emergency Management Agency
http://www.fema.gov

International Association of Fire Chiefs
http://www.ichiefs.org

International City/County Management Association
http://icma.org

International Critical Incident Stress Foundation
http://www.icisf.org

National Association of Counties
http://www.naco.org

National Disaster Medical System
Office of Emergency Preparedness
U.S. Department of Health and Human Services
http://www.oep-ndms.dhhs.gov/ndms/ndms.html

National Domestic Preparedness Office
Federal Bureau of Investigation
U.S. Department of Justice
http://www.fas.gov/irp/agency/doj/fbi/ndpo

National Fire Academy
Federal Emergency Management Agency
http://www.usfa.fema.gov

National Infrastructure Protection Center
http://www.nipc.gov

National Institute of Justice
U.S. Department of Justice
http://www.ojp.usdoj.gov/nij

National Medical Disaster System
Office of Emergency Preparedness
U.S. Public Health Service
http://ndms.dhhs.gov

National Security Agency
http://www.nsa.gov

Office for Victims of Crime
U.S. Department of Justice
http://www.ojp.usdoj/gov/ovc

Office of Domestic Preparedness
Office of Justice Programs
U.S. Department of Justice
http://osldps.ncjrs.org

Office of Homeland Security
Office of the President
U.S. Federal Government
http://www.whitehouse.gov/homeland

Operation Noble Eagle
U.S. Air Force
http://www.af.mil/news/efreedom

Public Entity Risk Institute
http://www.riskinstitute.org

Public Health Emergency Preparedness & Response
Centers for Disease Control and Prevention
U.S. Department of Health and Human Services
http://www.bt.cdc.gov

The Terrorism Research Center
http://www.terrorism.com

The War on Terrorism
Central Intelligence Agency
http://www.odci.gov/terrorism

U.S. Conference of Mayors
http://www.usmayors.org

U.S. Department of Defense
http://www.defenselink.mil

U.S. Department of Energy
http://www.energy.gov

U.S. Department of Health and Human Services
http://www.hhs.gov

U.S. Department of Justice
http://www.usdoj.gov

U.S. Department of State
http://www.state.gov

U.S. Environmental Protection Agency
http://www.epa.gov

Appendix G

Department of Homeland Security

Following are the agencies that are being transferred into the Department of Homeland Security. Their former departments are shown in the second column.

Border and Transportation Security

U.S. Customs Service	Treasury
The Immigration and Naturalization Service (part)	Justice
The Federal Protective Service	General Services Administration
The Transportation Security Administration	Transportation
Federal Law Enforcement Training Center	Treasury
Animal and Plant Health Inspection Service (part)	Agriculture
Office for Domestic Preparedness	Justice

Emergency Preparedness and Response

The Federal Emergency Management Agency	Independent
Strategic National Stockpile	Health/Human Services
National Disaster Medical System	Health/Human Services
Nuclear Incident ResponseTeam	Energy
Domestic Emergency Support Team	Justice
National Domestic Preparedness Office	FBI

Science and Technology

CBRN Countermeasures Programs	Energy
Environmental Measurements Laboratory	Energy
National BW Defense Analysis Center	Defense
Plum Island Animal Disease Center	Agriculture

Information Analysis and Infrastructure Protection

Critical Infrastructure Assurance Office	Commerce
Federal Computer Incident Response Center	General Services Administration
National Communications System	Defense
National Infrastructure Protection Center	FBI
Energy Security and Assurance Program	Energy

Secret Service

Coast Guard

Source: Department of Homeland Security, www.dhs.gov, March 2003.

Appendix H

Local response to homeland security advisory: Meriden, Connecticut

Note: The following information was prepared at a time when the level of security was heightened from code yellow to code orange under the Homeland Security Advisory System. When the code orange alert was announced, the Meriden city manager asked selected department heads and emergency personnel what they were doing differently under code orange compared with the previous code yellow. The resulting document represents the results of many hours of work on everyone's part. The information was distributed to the mayor and city council, all department managers, emergency management personnel, and the board of education. It was also posted on the city's web site, published by both local newspapers, placed as a public service message on the city's public-access cable television channel, and sent to the State league of cities to use as a model for others.

The City of Meriden's public officials are in constant contact with Federal and State agencies regarding National Alerts issued in response to anticipated terrorist activities in the United States. Representatives of the City's Police and Fire Departments, Health and Human Services Department, and Parks and Public Works Department are in constant contact with the City Manager, as well as the City's Emergency Management Coordinators. They meet periodically to discuss the City's response and to ensure that appropriate measures are being taken in response to the ongoing alert status.

Citizens should know that the City's Emergency Operations Center (EOC) can become operational at a moment's notice. The City also has a backup EOC should the primary one not be operational. While the City's Dispatching Center is located at the Police Department, its backup Dispatching Center would be located at the Fire Station on Pratt Street. The City's Primary Emergency Shelter is located at the Senior Citizens Center on West Main Street.

Actions being taken by the City, as well as recommended precautions for citizens and business persons, are categorically highlighted below.

Under the current *Code Orange Alert*, the City of Meriden will:

- Maintain a heightened sense of awareness while responding to, or working at, incident scenes.
- Review local emergency response plans and the Meriden Emergency Operations Plan.
- Communicate and coordinate with local law enforcement, emergency management, public health, public works, and other agencies to review their roles and responsibilities.
- Closely monitor available security and intelligence data from State and local law enforcement agencies.
- Inspect buildings and parking areas for suspicious packages.

- Instruct employees to be especially watchful for suspicious or unattended packages and articles received through the mail service.
- Consider controlled access to government buildings, critical facilities, and critical public infrastructure.
- Ensure appropriate security measures are in place and functioning properly.
- Increase monitoring of municipal reservoirs and watershed areas.
- Increase surveillance of all transmittable diseases.

Citizens are advised to consider the following under a *Code Orange Alert:*

- Resume normal activities but expect some delays, baggage searches, and restrictions as a result of heightened security at public buildings and facilities.
- Continue to monitor world and local events as well as local government threat advisory warnings.
- Report all suspicious activities at or near critical facilities to local law enforcement agencies by calling 9-1-1.
- Avoid leaving unattended packages or brief cases in public areas.
- Inventory and organize emergency supply kits and discuss emergency plans with family members. Reevaluate meeting location based on the national threat level.
- Consider taking reasonable personal security precautions. Be alert to your surroundings, avoid placing yourself in a vulnerable situation, and monitor the activities of your children.
- Maintain close contact with your family and neighbors to ensure their safety and emotional well-being.

Businesses should consider the following under a *Code Orange Alert:*

- Announce Threat Condition HIGH to all employees and explain expected actions.
- Place emergency response teams on notice.
- Activate the operations center if required.
- Monitor world and local events. Pass on credible threat intelligence to key personnel.
- Ensure appropriate security measures are in place and functioning properly.
- Instruct employees to report suspicious activities, packages, and people.
- Search all personal bags and parcels, and require personnel to pass through a metal detector, if available.
- Restrict vehicle parking close to buildings.
- Inspect intrusion detection systems and lighting, security fencing, and locking systems.
- Inspect all deliveries and consider accepting shipments only at off-site locations.
- Remind employees of security and evacuation procedures at current level, and continue all measures implemented from lower threat levels.
- Remind employees to expect delays and baggage searches.

City of Meriden officials feel these actions represent a reasonable and responsible approach based on the City's location and lack of potential strategic targets for terrorism. We will remain vigilant and prepared to respond to specific incidents should they occur.

Homeland Security-Related Web Sites

Department of Homeland Security
U.S. Government
http://www.dhs.gov/dhspublic

Federal Emergency Management Agency
U.S. Government
http://www.fema.gov

Office of Emergency Management
State of Connecticut
http://www.mil.state.ct.us/oem

Department of Public Health
State of Connecticut
http://www.dph.state.ct.us

American Red Cross
http://www.redcross.org

City of Meriden
http://www.cityofmeriden.org

Index